▶▶▶▶▶▶ Cinema One

19 Orson Welles

Orson Welles

Joseph McBride

New York

The Viking Press

The Cinema One series is published by
The Viking Press, Inc., in association with
the British Film Institute

Published in 1972 in a hardbound and paperbound
edition by
The Viking Press, Inc.
625 Madison Avenue, New York,
N.Y. 10022

SBN 670-52893-5 (hardbound)
     670-01937-2 (paperbound)

Library of Congress catalog card number: 70-178854

Printed and bound in Great Britain

Contents

Cover: Welles in *The Immortal Story*

1: Introduction: A Citizen of the Screen

'Orson Welles is an animal made for the screen and the stage.
When he steps before a camera, it is as if the rest of the world
ceases to exist. He is a citizen of the screen.'

Jean Renoir

I had the good fortune recently to take a premature look at the story
which will appear all over the world, under the auspices of a major
wire service, when Orson Welles dies. Newspapers keep these
instant obituaries on file for every celebrity, but Welles's holds a
special fascination. After all, his first act in his first feature film,
Citizen Kane, was to die, and most of his other films begin with
intimations of that strange moment in which a legendary life becomes a lifeless legend. Welles's obituary begins by calling him a
twentieth-century Alexander the Great, for ever seeking new worlds
to conquer, and then launches into a long account of the incident
which made him legendary, *The War of the Worlds*, his 1938 radio
show which fooled the country into thinking that the Martians were
invading. Legend is only peripherally concerned with fact, and the
obituary does not indicate that the show's effect was due largely to
peculiarities of timing; it was considered below the standard of his
best radio work. The account continues undaunted for seventeen
paragraphs, finally veering off for a sketchy summary of the 'boy
wonder's' career in movies and theatre, and from there into brief
biographical notes. What posterity will be concerned with, if it pays
no heed to the ghostly record of Welles's films, is the mere
mechanics of legend, the events leading up to the drama, not the
drama itself.

Welles has done nothing to discourage his popular role as a
demonic practical joker, and turned up on television recently to
announce, with almost bemused pride, 'Yes, ladies and gentlemen, I
was The Shadow,' referring to a radio programme in which he
played a spectral avenger of evil. The ironies proliferate – playing a

7

spirit in a medium of sounds is an extraordinarily theatrical venture – and if the emphasis on these early feats of legerdemain might seem misplaced next to the more substantial achievements of Welles's maturity, we can hardly help but realize that the creation of such a legend is central not only to Welles's *persona* but also to the deepest sources of his creative power. Welles has always been larger than life. Consider, for example, his attitude towards his birthplace, the prosaic Midwestern town of Kenosha, Wisconsin. Since he was conceived in Paris and named in Rio de Jañeiro, he believes that emerging in Kenosha was a gross injustice.

Consider his corpulence: he has called himself 'a rather over-fed Gandhi', and delighted in slimming down to play Falstaff. Or the question of a 'false face': when he was a small boy he carried his make-up kit to school and amused himself with it at recess. Once, to frighten off a bully, he painted a bloody face on himself. At the age of nine he made himself up as Lear. He has appeared only once in films without make-up, as Harry Lime in *The Third Man*, significantly enough the character he most detests of all those he has played. 'I hate Harry Lime,' he once said. 'He has no passion; he is cold; he is Lucifer, the fallen angel.' Welles keeps a collection of all the false noses he has ever worn, and has even worn them on the street.

The assumption of a false face is a necessary ritual for the Welles hero. He has a 'secret,' something to hide, like Adam hiding his nakedness. The climax in a Welles film is the unmasking of the hero by a younger man, who sees in the hero's face the shame of guilt and corruption, and thus is able to recognize it in himself. Self-deception and the struggle against awareness is the theme of Welles's films. And as Pierre Duboeuf has astutely observed, even in the naked face of Welles there is 'a certain irritation in the movement of his eyebrows, the sometimes extreme tension of his gaze, or some hesitation in the character's behaviour' that gives 'a pathetic dimension . . . a sense of fragility.'

The theatricality implicit in Welles's self-consciously humorous attitude towards himself leads some observers to rather outraged moral judgements. I have heard it said, for example, that Welles has no right to complain about inadequate financing for his films, since he probably eats away the equivalent of a feature film budget each year. If we would take such comments seriously, we might be compelled to see Welles as another Hemingway, losing sight of the

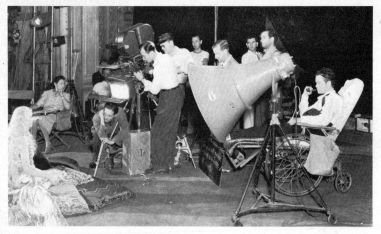

Citizen Kane: Welles on set in wheelchair

vulnerability underlying his heroes' protestations of strength and letting his personal re-enactment of their fantasies finally slip over, unqualified, into his work. But however exuberant Welles may be in playing himself to the public eye, in his work he has never ceased to maintain a complex ironic attitude towards his heroes. The youngster who painted faces on himself was also, we are told, quiet and self-effacing around other children. Hemingway took refuge from his fears by taking manly trips to the north woods with his father; Welles accompanied his *bon vivant* father on jaunts around the world, but felt just as close to his mother, a concert pianist, confidante of Ravel and Stravinsky. Beatrice Welles died when Orson was eight and Richard when he was thirteen. However tempting it may be, though, to see Welles as a homeless, vulnerable excursionist into worlds of magical, self-serving fantasy, the ultimate truth of his obsessions lies elsewhere.

Perhaps the key to Welles's personality is a statement he made recently while assessing his work: he described himself as 'a moralist against morality'. In the same interview, he elaborated: 'In reality, I am a man of ideas; yes, above all else – I am even more a man of ideas than a moralist, I suppose.' It is clear that Welles's films are not moralistic in the sense that Howard Hawks's are, for example – as fables of exemplary behaviour; and just as clearly, they are not anarchistic and behaviouristic like Jean Renoir's. In a Welles film there is, for the most part, an extreme dissonance between the characters' actions and emotions and the underlying moral framework.

Welles will be as chivalrous to his characters as Renoir, but he will not allow the characters' actions to determine the form of the film. Instead, he will go so far as to construct a geometrical pattern of counterpoints and visual ironies, in *Kane*, to bind his hero into a system which makes him seem, from our contemplative vantage point, almost powerless. Or, in *The Magnificent Ambersons* and most of his later films, he will use a godlike narrator to detach us from the struggles of the hero; in most of his films he distorts chronological structure, beginning the film with scenes which depict or imply the hero's destruction, thus placing his subsequent actions in an ironic parenthesis. His opening scenes often contain a poetic or literal 'synopsis' of the story which is to follow. *Kane* has its newsreel, *The Ambersons* its quasi-documentary on the town, *Macbeth* the witches' convocation, *Othello* its funeral procession and caging of Iago, *The Trial* its parable of the law, *Chimes at Midnight* the conversation between the two old men, Falstaff and Shallow, recounting their lives. These overviews serve a function similar in some ways to that of the chorus in a Greek tragedy: acquainting us with the broad outlines of the myth so that we will be aware of the consequences inherent in the hero's actions *as* he carries them out, and placing us in an exalted moral position which enables us to maintain a concurrent emotional sympathy and ideological detachment.

We should not suppose, however, that Welles is a determinist. The structural similarity to Greek tragedy, and the resulting evocation of a dimly realized fate which becomes clear to the hero only at the moment of destruction, should not obscure the deeper allegiances of his moral position. The 'fate' metaphor is not the core of his position; it is a framework, a device which throws the hero's true responsibilities into relief. Welles is a deeply rhetorical artist, but an ironist, not a propagandist. In *The Trial*, for example, he seems to be making the best possible case for the worst character he can imagine as still capable of heroism. Kane is most charming at his most morally odious moments – starting a war, harassing innocent citizens with captivating arrogance – and most pathetic in his moments of tenderness. We can see that power, intellect, and charm come so easily to Welles himself that he tends to view them less as virtues than as moral temptations, but there is an even more sinister cast to this duplicity. Beyond masking an inability to lead a simple, stable emotional life, power and its attendant anxieties tend to plague the Welles hero past the point of futile compensation into the realm of gratuitous brutality. And with this comes a horrible sense of guilt – not the sentimental regret for being less than perfect, but the knowledge that emotional vulnerability has been the excuse for endlessly enlarging malignity, an obsession which thrusts its cause deeper and deeper into the subconscious and necessitates a greater and greater hypocrisy.

The creation of myth is not only a means by which the Welles hero conceals his moral weakness from himself and others; it is also the creation of a more easily manageable rationale for his actions. Kane justifies his abuse of friendship with his self-sufficiency as a legend, but underneath this is a deeper cause he will not admit, and which finally destroys him. He deludes himself into thinking that he has become a prisoner to his legend, and no longer personally responsible (the sense of determinism), just as Joseph K. in *The Trial* excuses himself as the victim of a universal conspiracy. It is only when the myth is exposed as sham that he comes to face the guilt within himself. The same pattern is repeated, with an increasingly melancholic self-awareness, for all of Welles's heroes, until in *Chimes at Midnight* the mask of deception becomes painfully candid. Falstaff is not only the hero of the tragedy; he seems to incorporate within himself the soul of the tragedian as well. He is a liar who expects no one to believe his lies, and so exaggerates them to the point of absurdity. The lies are no longer lies but a desperate confession.

And if *The Immortal Story* seems both the most intimately personal and the most theatrical work of Welles's career, the paradox is inevitable. Welles is the most theatrical of film directors, even more so than Cukor, Ophüls, or Bergman. His dual presence as both author and hero is all but essential to his work. *The Trial* suffers because of an excessive and stifling distance between Welles and his hero; Welles appears in the film as the hero's nemesis, and the moral rhetoric involved almost swamps any possibility of sympathy with the hero. In *The Magnificent Ambersons*, his only feature film in which he does not appear, the hero closely resembles Welles, and the metamorphosis is immeasurably smoother. When Welles appears on the screen, he feels the necessity to surround himself with baroque distortions of the real world. The time is out of joint the moment he steps on. And we always know the source of the distortion; from the very beginnings of his career, Welles has flaunted his command of his media. In his puppet theatre plays, he would supply the voices of all the characters himself. An idle boy's amusement? In *The Trial* Welles not only plays the Advocate but narrates the film and dubs in the voices of eleven other characters, creating an eerie sense of omnipresence. In his radio plays he would often interrupt the narrative to make comments both on the characters and on the medium itself. Time and again on the stage he dramatized his position as cosmic ringmaster; when he did a musical version of *Around the World in Eighty Days*, he trotted out a kitchen sink just to prove that he had not forgotten.

Throughout his films, the moral presence of Welles makes itself felt through the eye of the camera. In a Welles film the camera is a character. In his script for *Heart of Darkness*, his first Hollywood project, this is literally true – the camera was to have been Marlow. In *Kane* the camera shadows the reporter, whose face we never see. The intricate camera movements and 'long takes' characteristic of Welles help to immerse us in the maze-like ironies of his scenes. The camera is the audience, and the longer it moves without the distancing device of a cut, the more we are made aware of its (our) shifting relationship to the characters. Welles comments: 'I believe, thinking about my films, that they are based not so much on pursuit as on a search. If we are looking for something, the labyrinth is the most favourable location for the search. I do not know why, but my films are all for the most part a physical search.' Perhaps because they are also a moral search, an inquiry by the audience into the truth about the legendary hero.

While retaining the freedom to use rapid montage for physical immediacy (as in the battle sequence of *Chimes at Midnight*) or for intellectual comment (as in the ending sequence of *Touch of Evil*), Welles tends to prolong the tension among the characters and camera as long as possible, to approximate the intimacy of a theatrical experience. The long take, like the deep-focus photography of which Welles is fond, helps persuade us of the dramatic reality of the scene – a necessary counterpoint to the moral distancing – and in respecting the integrity of time and space, it asserts the moral unity of what is shown. Though the event, for example the long uninterrupted snow scene in *Kane* or the tortuous interrogation scenes in *Touch of Evil*, may be highly dialectical in emotions and ideas, the integrality of the *mise-en-scène* functions as a metaphor for the inevitability of the actions' coincidence. The camera creates a moral labyrinth in which the characters must struggle, ironically unaware of the depth of their dilemma. An excellent example is the long dolly shot in *The Ambersons* moving along with George and Lucy as they argue in their carriage. We see the characters' feelings ('identify' with them), but the ceaseless variation of the distance between the camera and the carriage also distances us from them. This distortion, a contrapuntal actor-camera movement, a montage *within* the shot, helps to explain the mixture of compassion and irony omnipresent in Welles's films.

If Welles is to be defined at all (and let's not, since the legacy of his films will surpass any obituary), it will have to be in terms of his contradictions. As his friend Jean Cocteau so memorably put it, 'Orson Welles is a giant with the face of a child, a tree filled with birds and shadows, a dog who has broken loose from his chains and gone to sleep on the flower-bed. He is an active loafer, a wise madman, a solitude surrounded by humanity . . .' From *Citizen Kane*, an examination into legend which finds the possibility of definition illusory, to *Chimes at Midnight* and *The Immortal Story*, which turn the idea of legend into a monstrous, melancholy *jeu d'esprit*, Welles has been enchanting us with the spectacle of a magnificent being exalting and deriding himself in a single stroke. In a world from which dinosaurs and emperors have vanished, a world for ever growing smaller, Orson Welles survives to share with us his boundless delight in being himself.

2: Meeting Orson Welles

'Ah, but Orson. Mostly, he's a child ... You worry very much when you love Orson, because you never know where he is. He disappears, you don't know where he is and it is nearly impossible to find him, because his life is always complicated ... And besides, that huge, strong man, you know that he's very easily loved, that he's very fragile, but it's very easy to hurt him ... so you love him and you want to protect him. And if he calls you and says, "I need you," then you say "Orson needs me and it's something important." His career is so strange because he's capable of such beautiful things and it's so hard for him now to make a film that you wouldn't be the little stone that would stop the machine from going, once he has the chance to make a film. I think that's why we all do react that way.'

Jeanne Moreau

Welles was always Somewhere in Europe during the four years I spent writing this book, so I never tried to arrange a meeting. But in the summer of 1970, when the book was virtually completed, I learned that he was in New York City. By the time my letter arrived, though, he was gone again. Then he was supposed to come to Chicago, but he didn't. I began to wonder if Orson Welles wasn't really a pseudonym for Howard Hughes. In August I went to Hollywood (surely the last place Welles would be) to interview John Ford and Jean Renoir, the other two of my three favourite directors. My stay was almost over when I learned that Welles was a couple of miles away, appearing on Dean Martin's television show.

So I picked up the phone and called him. He invited me for lunch and mentioned that he was about to start shooting a new film, *The Other Side of the Wind*. Would I like to be in it? Flabbergasted, I said of course, it would be wonderful. He explained that he would be taking a troupe down to Tijuana on Sunday afternoon to film scenes of the hero, an ageing movie director, watching the bullfights with some of his young admirers – 'test scenes' to help him raise enough money to complete the film. I remembered that Welles had wanted to make a similar story, called *The Sacred Beasts*, several years before. This would be a 'permutation' of the earlier script, he said.

After spending an evening discussing the mysteries of Welles's career with Peter Bogdanovich, the young writer-director who is

'. . . like a polar bear.' Welles in Los Angeles, summer 1970

collaborating with him on an interview book entitled *This Is Orson Welles*, I went to Welles's rented house high in the Los Angeles hills. He was typing in the foyer, swathed in a massive white silk dressing-gown that made him look like a polar bear. I was waiting to hear his laugh – that immense, intimidating, chilling laugh so familiar from the screen – but when it came, I was surprised. When Welles laughs, he starts slowly, cocking an eye towards his companion, watching his response. When the response is encouraging (how couldn't it be?), the laugh swells and begins to gather force, like a typhoon, until his features are dissolved into a mask of Falstaffian delight. Still, the laugh is ingratiating, not intimidating, for Welles keeps a slight portion of that eye fixed on his companion.

Visitors were offered Wellesian cigars (seven inches long, by my measure) from a box on the piano. When there was temerity, Welles would insist. Soon there would be four or five miniature Orsons trundling around the house. I lit one and sat down to talk with a man who, a few hours before, I had known only as a figure of legend.

Welles had a good time puncturing my illusions. He poked fun at

15

me for being so absorbed in movies. 'I've never been excited by movies *as movies* the way I've been excited by magic or bullfighting or painting,' he said. 'After all, the world existed for a long time without people going to movies.' I said that he had given his life to movies, but I could see that it was the other way around: movies have only served to give him to us.

We talked for a while about the endless vagaries of production and distribution, and then he brought another of my fancies down to earth. I asked him why, in recent years, his movies have had less and less of the razzle-dazzle of his youth. Could it be a kind of growing serenity? 'No, the explanation is simple,' he said. 'All the great technicians are dead or dying. You can't get the kind of boom operator I had, for example, on *Touch of Evil*. That man, John Russell, is now a lighting cameraman. I have to make do with what I can get.' So much, I suppose, for my theory, but *tant pis* anyway.

Watching Welles work the next day, I realized something about him I had known but had never really understood. He genuinely lives for the moment. Though he takes great care with each detail of his work, he jumps at every chance to add something new, something unexpected, to his prior conceptions. 'Movies should be rough,' he told me. I asked if he had been working on the script of *The Other Side of the Wind* when I had walked in. He laughed and said there wasn't any script, the film would be improvised. Seeing my surprise, he said that he had written a script which would have run for nine hours on the screen, but had put it aside because he realized that he was writing a novel. 'I'm going to improvise out of everything I know about the characters and the situation,' he said. He had a large cardboard box crammed with notes sitting next to his typewriter.

I was restless in my hotel that night. My only previous 'acting' experience had been a walk-on in one of my own films which was flubbed because I had misjudged the depth of field and walked so close to the lens that I came out as a blur. I had also appeared in two *cinéma-vérité* films, the Leacock–Pennebaker–Maysles *Primary* and Robin Spry's *Prologue*, but those were records of big political events (a Jack Kennedy speech, the Chicago convention) at which I was a spectator. I suppose I should have been terrified, but all I could think about was how much fun it was going to be.

Shooting in Tijuana was impossible, I learned the next day,

because of some government edict against taking cameras across the border. So we gathered at Welles's house to shoot a birthday party at which the director-hero, Jake Hannaford, is besieged by the myrmidons of the media. 'The joke is that the media are feeding off him,' Welles explained, 'but they end up feeding off themselves. It's sort of his last summer. That's what it's all about.' Welles sat down with Bogdanovich and me and two other young *cinéastes*, Eric Sherman and Felipe Herba, who had also been recruited for the film. Welles brimmed over with amusement as he told us about our roles – Bogdanovich would be a foundation-backed hustler following Hannaford around doing an interview book; I would be a pompous cinema aesthete spouting blather from my book about Hannaford; and Sherman and Herba would be a blasé *cinéma-vérité* crew ('the Maysles brothers', Welles called them) doing a documentary about the great man. Welles said he did not yet know who would play Hannaford; so our scenes today would be shot with the hero off-screen (which would certainly help point up the isolation of the man from his sycophants).

Welles asked Bogdanovich and me to start throwing him fatuous questions which we could use in the film. Bogdanovich asked if his character should be effeminate, and it was decided that no, he should be excitable, like Jerry Lewis. So he began quacking away like Lewis, and Welles toned the voice down here, broadened it there, parrying the lines back and forth with him. I mentioned a pet theory I had about Ford, how his films since 1939 can be taken as an oblique reflection on the changes in American society, and Welles quizzed me on how I would develop it, warning me to keep it fairly straight. He finally went to the typewriter and we concocted a speech (Welles supplying the final wording): 'The main thrust of my argument, you understand, is that during the Thirties Hannaford's predominant motif was the outsider in absurd conflict with society. In the Forties he achieved salvation. In the Fifties . . .' Here Bogdanovich would break in with, 'Never mind the Fifties. Open the whisky bottle.' Welles roared with delight; so much for the critics!

We spent half an hour thinking up these ridiculous questions. Once, when I suggested asking Hannaford about the work of Dziga Vertov, Welles said, 'You're kidding! Who's that?' 'Dziga Vertov, the Russian director of the 1920s,' I replied. 'He made newsreels known as *Kino-Pravda*.' Welles had a great time with that one

Gary Graver ('Rembrandt'), cameraman on *The Other Side of the Wind*

before ruling me out of order. 'Come on, now,' he said. 'You're supposed to be playing a serious character.' We did wind up with a Godardian-Vertovian question, though. I would ask Hannaford, while riding in the back seat of his car, 'Mr Hannaford, is the camera eye a reflection of reality, or is reality a reflection of the camera eye? Or is the camera a phallus?'

I was beginning fully to appreciate Welles's sense of humour, which is sometimes submerged under the rhetorical cocoon surrounding his characters and usually fails to emerge from an analysis of his films. And when the shooting started, I could see first-hand the delight he takes in the physical act of direction. His young crew officially numbered four, but eventually all twelve people present pitched in to help, and almost everybody appeared before the camera, including Welles's houseboy.

It seemed that what Welles was shooting today – brief, fairly simple hand-held shots – was pure caviar to the director. I quickly realized that I couldn't be either good or bad, just myself, because the character I was playing was a fool. Comic relief was the order of the day, and Welles's brio belied the idea that directing comedy is a dour business. It certainly was hard work, though. 'Now you appreciate what actors go through,' Welles told me when I sighed after the seventh take of one shot went wrong. Since I was the buffoon among buffoons, I was loaded to the teeth with props – a tape-recorder, a still camera, a coat over my arm, papers in my shirt pocket, and a gigantic whisky bottle. I apologized for my awkwardness with the props, and Welles said reassuringly that the only actor he ever knew who could handle so many props well was Erich von Stroheim. Adding to my surrealistic appearance was something Bogdanovich had noticed the night I went to his house – I had been without notepaper that day at a screening of Fellini's *Satyricon*, and had scribbled some notes on my wrist in the dark. Welles told me that, in the film, I should have my wrist and arm covered with notes – 'Oedipus Complex', 'Mother Fixation', and so forth. When the shooting was over, he paternally insisted that I scrub my wrist and arm completely clean, even though I was too tired to lift a bar of soap.

In twelve hours of shooting, Welles completed twenty-seven shots. It was fascinating to watch him sculpt each shot from the bare bones of dialogue. For example, the pontificating about Hannaford in the different decades of his career was broken into two shots, the second of which required fourteen takes. I began to understand what Welles once said about his direction of actors: 'I give them a great deal of freedom and, at the same time, the feeling of precision. It's a strange combination. In other words, physically, and in the way they develop, I demand the precision of ballet. But their way of acting comes directly from their own ideas as much as from mine. When the camera begins to roll, I do not improvise visually. In this realm, everything is prepared. But I work very freely with the actors. I try to make their life pleasant.' Setting up the first shot for the scene, Welles chose a stark wall, couch, and table for the background. Because the setting was a party, with cameramen's lights present, the lighting was not to be over-refined. Directing from a throne-like chair at the typewriter table ('because this is an *auteur* film'), Welles took an active part in the lighting, ordering his cameraman, Gary Graver, to forget about an elaborate cross-lighting pattern he had set up when the director wasn't looking. But he did tell Graver to set up a light behind a bedroom door in the background so it would cast a serrated pattern on the floor. 'That's the only beautiful thing I want in the shot,' he said. Then, turning to Bogdanovich with an arch expression, he muttered, 'Von Sternberg...' Welles ran quickly and efficiently through the

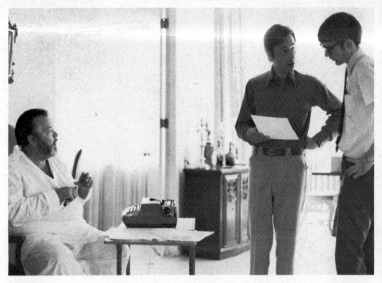

'The thespians are causing trouble . . .' Welles, Peter Bogdanovich and Joseph McBride

lighting, keeping Graver (whom he called 'Rembrandt') constantly on the move.

Bogdanovich and I were rehearsing our lines, and Welles interrupted us to give directions. The scene would begin with an offscreen hand giving Bogdanovich the whisky bottle from camera left, and bits of dialogue were added, to be spoken while I was talking. (When someone broke into the shooting of another scene to tell Welles that there was overlapping dialogue, he replied, 'We *always* have overlapping dialogue.') Bogdanovich would disdainfully ignore me while I was talking. When I would say 'during the Thirties . . .' he would give me the bottle, taking my tape-recorder, and tell me to open the bottle. I would ask, 'How?' In the meantime, the houseboy (standing in the background wearing a camera around his neck and munching a chicken breast) would slowly cross in front of us, and Bogdanovich would ask him, 'Where's Andy?' The question would go unanswered – the houseboy would act stoned.

Then Bogdanovich would tell me, 'There's a cork, isn't there?' and I would look down and find no cork on the bottle. The Maysles brothers, who would be chattering in the background all the while, would now run like hell behind us with their equipment in search of a shot. I would resume my talking, and the Maysles's assistant (actually Graver's assistant) would dash *between* us holding a still camera and a blazing sun-gun, chasing after them. Bogdanovich would then interrupt me ('part Jerry and part Noël Coward', Welles told him) with, 'Never mind the Fifties. Open the whisky bottle.' In addition to all this, the tape flew off my recorder when I handed it to Bogdanovich during a run-through, and Welles insisted on keeping the action in the film. So we rehearsed dropping the tape.

Finally, we were ready to go. The first part of the scene – up to the exchange of the bottle and the tape-recorder – went fairly quickly. Welles said he would cut to an insert of some kind and return to the same shot of Bogdanovich and me from the knees up. We began to shoot the second part of the scene. Chaos. I would bobble my lines, Bogdanovich would react too slowly, the guy eating the chicken would take too long in getting past us, the Maysles brothers would run through at the wrong time... After several takes fell completely flat, all of a sudden one of them worked. But in a rhythm totally different from what Welles had planned. All the cues were different, but it seemed to jell anyway. Welles said he might wind up using the shot, but would appreciate it if we'd try it again, *his* way. Bogdanovich and I started to chatter about ways to improve the shot. Welles ordered quiet. 'The *thespians* are causing trouble,' he said. 'What do you want?' Cowed, we fell silent. 'All right, then,' he said. 'Let's do it again, shall we?' About an hour later, we were done.

The rest of the day was taken up with scenes of the media people assembled in various parts of the house, thrusting equipment forward at Hannaford, and with some hilarious scenes inside and outside a car moving through the streets of Los Angeles and Beverly Hills. Welles told us to leave without him to shoot the scenes inside the car because it would be more interesting if we'd spring the results on him after following his instructions. 'I did that with one scene in *Touch of Evil*,' he recalled. 'Remember that wide-angle shot of the two men driving through the street? There was no sound man, no cameraman, and no director.' Where was the camera? I asked. 'Strapped to the hood of the car,' he said with a triumphant grin.

Welles, Peter Bogdanovich and cat during the shooting of *The Other Side of the Wind*

Relaxing aboard a home-bound jet that night, I began to think back on recent events. Four days earlier, Renoir had told me that to learn about directing, I should try a little bit of acting (he meant in an amateur movie). Now I had ceased looking over Welles's shoulder and had begun looking directly into his eyes. My subject had climbed down off the pedestal I had built for him and, curiously, he now seemed larger than ever. As his cameraman said admiringly after the day's shooting, 'Welles doesn't play it safe.'

3: Apprentice Work

Welles has never mentioned to interviewers that he did any experimentation in film before coming to Hollywood, undoubtedly preferring the world to think that he burst full-blown on the scene with *Citizen Kane*. To an interviewer who asked him recently how he arrived at *Kane's* 'cinematic innovations', he replied airily, 'I owe it to my ignorance. If this word seems inadequate to you, replace it with innocence.' But Welles was not really a filmic innocent. There have been a few furtive mentions, largely unheeded by film historians, of a film he shot in 1938 for use in a Mercury Theatre stage production, William Gillette's farce *Too Much Johnson*. The film was never shown publicly because Welles decided not to bring the play to Broadway after a summer stock try-out. He reportedly shot a twenty-minute silent prologue to the play, and ten-minute films to introduce the second and third acts. Included in the cast were Joseph Cotten, Edgar Barrier, Marc Blitzstein, and Virginia Nicholson, Welles's first wife. The story concerned an 1890s New York rake chased to Cuba by his mistress's husband.

Sadly, the only copy of the film was destroyed in an August 1970 fire at Welles's villa in Madrid which also consumed several unpublished books and unproduced scripts. Welles was sanguine about the loss when I met him three weeks later. 'It's probably a good thing,' he said. 'I never cared much for possessions, but over the years I accumulated a few. Now I can tell everybody how great those scripts were! I wish you could have seen *Too Much Johnson*, though. It was a beautiful film. We created a sort of dream Cuba in New York. I looked at it four years ago and the print was in wonderful condition. You know, I never edited it. I meant to put it together to

give to Joe Cotten as a Christmas present one year, but I never got around to it.' He also shot a film as prologue to his 1939 vaudeville show, *The Green Goddess*, 'depicting an air crash in the Himalayas', according to his associate Richard Wilson. Its whereabouts is unknown.

But I have been able to unearth an extremely interesting little silent film called *The Hearts of Age*, preserved in a private collection, which was Welles's first venture into film. It runs about four minutes and stars Welles and Virginia Nicholson. The copy I saw, until recently probably the only one extant, was the original 16 mm print. It was donated, as part of the Vance collection, to the Greenwich (Conn.) Public Library. The sound of the splices clicking through the projector was nerve-racking – though the film is in remarkably good condition – but my apprehension about projecting it was more than assuaged by the excitement of discovery. Access to the film has now been given to the American Film Institute, and a duplicate negative for preservation is lodged in the Library of Congress, which has also made a study copy which can be viewed by scholars on Library premises. (A study copy can likewise be seen at the Greenwich Library.)

The credit cards list only the title and the actors, but they are in Welles's handwriting. The film was made in the summer of 1934, when he was nineteen, at the drama festival he sponsored at the

Too Much Johnson: (*left*) Welles in straw hat directing Joseph Cotten; (*above*) instant Cuba, with John Houseman on ground

Todd School in Woodstock, Illinois, from which he had been graduated three years before. It was co-directed by William Vance, who produced it and makes a brief appearance. The late Mr Vance was a college student when he met Welles; he later went on to produce and direct television commercials. I saw a ten-minute adaptation of *Dr Jekyll and Mr Hyde*, made in 1932, which he stars in and directed. It is nothing more than a crude and rather risible student movie. *The Hearts of Age* is something more, however. Although Welles told me it could hardly be considered directorial experience, since it was just 'a Sunday afternoon home movie', there are many flourishes which point unmistakably to his later work. A few of the shots are eerily prophetic of *Kane*, and the film shows even more than *Kane* the extent to which Welles was under the spell of German theatrical and cinematic expressionism. If some of the camerawork is perfunctory (especially when Welles is not on the screen), many of the shots are beautifully lit and composed, and the general lack of coherence is almost offset by the humour of Welles's performance.

Welles poked gentle fun at me for taking the film seriously, since it was intended, he said, as a rib on *Blood of a Poet* and the whole surrealist school. The character he plays is an old man, apparently a figure of death, and I had taken this to be a foreshadowing of his later fascination with age and corruption. But there was a simpler explanation; he was copying the appearance of the doctor in *The Cabinet of Dr Caligari*. In any case, the film belongs in the same genre as the 'serious' avant-garde shorts of the period. The surrealist movement was itself largely a joke against respectable art, and it's often impossible to draw the line between pretension and put-on in a film such as Man Ray's *Les Mystères du Château du Dé*. It would be foolish to try to discuss *The Hearts of Age* as anything but juvenilia, but it does show a vigorous, unguarded, *personal* approach even in its facetious steals from other movies. *Citizen Kane*, we should remember, is also the product of youthful eclecticism. That is part of its charm; its strength, like that of the first *nouvelle vague* films, comes from the integration of these divergent styles into a coherent framework, each part appropriate to the drama. We can see in *The Hearts of Age* that Welles, like many young artists, had to work a penchant for playful in-joking out of his system before being able to create a unified work.

At first the film seems hopelessly muddled. The first shot is of a spinning Christmas tree ball (*Kane!*), which is later repeated and then echoed again when a white-robed figure walks past stroking a globe. After the opening shot, we see a quick montage (much too quick for comfort, with that projector churning away) of bells ringing, some of the shots in negative (the influence of F. W. Murnau's *Nosferatu*). Then we see an old lady – Virginia Nicholson in grotesque make-up – rocking back and forth. The camera, smoothly hand-held in contrast to the jerky camerawork in *Dr Jekyll*, pulls slowly back to show that she is suggestively straddling a ringing bell. The next shots reveal a man in black-face, wigged and dressed in lacy little boy's costume incongruously completed by football knickers, pulling the bell-rope, with the old lady on the roof above him. After the second shot of the spinning ball, we see a tilted shot of a gravestone with three elongated shadows moving slowly on the ground behind it, and then a grave marker tilted in the opposite direction with a hand grasped around it.

A shadow hand rings a shadow bell, hazy latticework lighting all around it; we are reminded that Welles, by the age of nineteen, had already directed and lit more than a score of plays, both with the Todd School's student company and in Dublin, where he had been an actor with the Gate and Abbey Players and a director at the Gate Studio. There is nothing in *Dr Jekyll* to compare with the suppleness of this film's lighting. The hand-bell falls harshly to the ground in the next shot, no longer a shadow now, and we return to the old lady riding the bell with an obscenely pained expression as the black-faced man tugs spiritedly away. She opens an umbrella over her head (Welles was also fond of Keaton, who liked to fool around with umbrellas when it wasn't raining). We see a hand spinning a globe in close-up, and then a striking shot, worthy of Murnau: a grey tombstone, dizzily tilted, with a shadow hand creeping up it (a *white* shadow, because the shot is in negative) and beckoning with a long finger, while a corporeal hand crawls along the edge of the stone. We see a piano keyboard – a flash-forward, as it turns out – and then Orson Welles opening a door over a rickety flight of stairs.

It is always a strange experience to stumble back upon the first screen appearance of one of the *monstres sacrés*. The shock of that first entrance is not only the shock of recognition, it is like a glimpse of a Platonic form. We are watching a privileged drama; every step, every gesture, is hazardous and exciting, because what is at stake is the formation of a legend. Sometimes we are startled, as when we see Chaplin without tramp's costume as a suave, top-hatted villain. Does he know what we know? Or are we witness to the very moments in which the great secret makes itself known? Enchanting to see Katharine Hepburn sweep down a staircase in *A Bill of Divorcement*, Cukor's camera whipping across an entire room to intercept her flight; but how would we react if we could see Garbo in the advertising film she made for a department store, demonstrating how not to dress? With a bravura that will come to be known as his, Welles the director delays Welles the actor from appearing until we are sufficiently expectant of a grand entrance, an apparition that will transfix our attention.

Whatever doubts we might have as to Welles's self-awareness are immediately dispelled by his appearance, mincing and leering, in a sort of comic Irishman costume, his face grotesquely aged like the lady's, his hairline masked and a wispy clown wig protruding from his temples. He starts down the stairs, bowing to the old lady. He carries a top-hat and a cane – later to be the talisman of other Wellesian characters, from Bannister in *The Lady from Shanghai* to Mr Clay in *The Immortal Story*. He descends the stairs from a variety of angles, intercut with the old lady watching warily. Then Welles shows the character walking down the steps three times in succession, a common enough affectation but appropriate here to underscore the fateful nature of the character's arrival. Presently we are treated to quick appearances of Miss Nicholson as a Keystone Cop and Mr Vance as an Indian wrapped in a blanket (making a face into the camera as he passes), neither of which has much connection with the already rather tenuous story.

It becomes clear that Welles's character is a death-figure, for he disturbs the indefatigably rocking old lady by appearing all over the rooftop of an adjoining building – and making a choking gesture with his cane for the man in black-face, a gesture echoed twenty-five years later by Quinlan in *Touch of Evil*. One of those quaint inserts dear to Griffith and Stroheim interrupts the action: a hand pouring coins from a shell, and a broom sweeping the money away. (Later we will see a hand dropping a crumpled five-dollar bill to the floor, but nothing else will come of it.) Death appears at the window, leering coyly and dangling two heart-shaped lollipops, tortuously wrapped around each other. These especially infuriate the old lady,

The Hearts of Age: Welles and Virginia Nicholson (frame enlargements)

who accelerates her rocking. From the smiling Death, Welles cuts to a skull, to a yanking rope, to a pair of feet hanging in mid-air, and to the head of the black-faced bellringer, dangling in a noose. Then we see a drawing of the hanged bellringer, and soon a hand enters the frame and draws a little bell as signature in the corner.

There is a startling transition to Death walking into a darkened room (the underworld?) carrying a candelabrum. He places it on a piano and starts to play, the camera tilted wildly to the right as he pounds furiously away: very much *The Phantom of the Opera*. We see his fingers coming closer and closer to the camera. Abruptly the pianist hits a wrong note and stops. He plunks at the keys, bending his head owlishly to test the sound (a good job of miming by Welles). He gets up and discovers that the old lady is lying dead inside the piano. Death opens the piano bench and takes out, instead of sheet music, a pile of thin slabs, shaped like tombstones. He shuffles through them: 'Sleeping', 'At Rest', 'In Peace', 'With the Lord', and 'The End', leaving the last behind. He sits down again to play, undulating deliriously. We see the bell again, and then his hands playing the piano. Then the slab, 'The End'.

After turning down a series of Hollywood offers because they did not offer him complete financial and artistic control, Welles signed with RKO Radio Pictures in 1939. Part of his purpose was to raise money for a revival of his catastrophic Shakespearean chronicle *Five Kings*, and he intended to return to Broadway after completing his first feature, an adaptation of Joseph Conrad's *Heart of Darkness* in which he would play Kurtz and the camera would play Marlow. He had written the script with John Houseman, his Mercury Theatre partner. Production was to begin in October 1939 (Welles had already shot some test scenes), but financial difficulties occasioned by the outbreak of the war in Europe, and the studio's qualms about the 'experimental' nature of the project, caused it to be shelved indefinitely. Probably the *coup de grâce* was the internment in France of the Austrian actress Dita Parlo, who was to have been the female lead.

Welles's forced inactivity occasioned much gloating from his enemies, who considered him a spoiled prodigy and objected both to his lucrative contract and to the beard he had grown for *Five Kings* and intended to wear in *Heart of Darkness*. The beard was the subject of a hilarious *Esquire* story by F. Scott Fitzgerald, who has his hero, a hack scriptwriter, explain: 'I wouldn't be surprised if Orson Welles is the biggest menace that's come to Hollywood for years. He gets a hundred and fifty grand a picture and I wouldn't be surprised if he was so radical that you had to have all new equipment and start all over again like you did with sound in 1928.' A stuntman cut off Welles's tie in a restaurant, and a press agent sent him a bearded ham for Christmas. He was angry. 'However unsuccessful my efforts,' he said, 'I can't have had much time for recreation.'

Besides writing scripts, he was broadcasting a weekly radio programme from Hollywood and giving himself a crash course in motion-picture technique. George J. Schaefer, the sympathetic president of RKO who was later purged with Welles in the débâcle of 1942, offered to let him make *Heart of Darkness* if he would first shoot, without salary, a film of Nicholas Blake's thriller *The Smiler with the Knife*. Welles and Houseman again wrote a script, only to find that several leading ladies, including Rosalind Russell and Carole Lombard, did not want to risk appearing for an untried director. Welles actually wanted to make the film without established stars, but Lucille Ball, his first choice, was also unavailable. So there the situation stood until he began work on *Citizen Kane*.

In the interim Welles had been running off scores of old films in Hollywood and at the Museum of Modern Art, and discussing each area of technique with the RKO craftsmen. Exhilarated by the panoply of studio machinery, he made a famous comment to Richard Wilson: 'This is the biggest electric train set any boy ever had!' The film which held his particular attention was John Ford's *Stagecoach*, released in 1939, a prototype for all later Westerns even if, notwithstanding its critical reputation, it does not approach the standard of Ford's later work. To an interviewer in 1963, Welles said: 'Who do I like? Griffith, Renoir, De Sica, Flaherty, Wajda, even some of the early Pagnol. Not "cinema" but something else, just as good. John Ford was my teacher. My own style has nothing to do with his, but *Stagecoach* was my movie textbook. I ran it over forty times.' To Kenneth Tynan in 1967, he was even more emphatic. He said that he liked 'the old masters. By which I mean John Ford, John Ford and John Ford. With Ford at his best, you feel that the movie has lived and breathed in a real world, even though it may have been written by Mother Machree.'

Though he is revered in Europe, Ford does not have the same critical following in America. Part of the problem, of course, is that his moral system, and the style which embodies it, are out of fashion; furthermore, he is action-oriented and unpretentious, and most American critics are culture-vultures. Like Welles himself, however, he is almost universally esteemed by other directors, particularly by directors who began in theatre. Ford's films have a pervasive personality, an invigorating blend of comedy and drama, nostalgia and adventure. In the absolute precision of his style, one senses a kind of incantatory force, the feeling of an order imposed on an instinctive action by a stylization that is both naturalistic and at a pitch removed from the naturalistic, an order corresponding at once to the real world and to an ideal world of which the precision of style is a mirror. Welles once said that he considered De Sica's *Shoeshine* the greatest film he had ever seen. 'In handling the camera I feel that I have no peer,' he explained. 'But what De Sica can do, that I can't do. I ran his *Shoeshine* again recently and the camera disappeared, the screen disappeared; it was just life . . .' However much he might value De Sica's style (and Jean Renoir's), Welles undoubtedly has been able to learn much more from Ford. Though there is little in *Stagecoach* that directly corresponds to Welles's work, there is a graceful amalgamation of theatricality and emotional simplicity towards which Welles will gradually work his way. And when he startlingly recreates a shot from *Stagecoach* thirty years later in *Chimes at Midnight*, not coincidentally a work with many echoes of Ford, the debt to his master will be paid.

4: Citizen Kane

'In one of the tales of Chesterton, *The Head of Caesar*, I believe, the hero observes that nothing is more frightening than a centreless labyrinth. This film is just like that labyrinth.'

Jorge Luis Borges

'Movies,' said Welles in 1970, 'should be rough.' But he began his movie career in 1940 by making a fanatically precise *objet d'art* which left not the tiniest detail to chance . . . *Citizen Kane*. It was the perfect mirror-image for a man of the theatre who had found himself world-famous at the age of twenty-three. Now was the time to explore the surfaces of illusion. The newspaper magnate Charles Foster Kane creates a world in his own image; when the image is shattered, nothing is left but vanity and death. *Kane* is ostensibly an attempt to resolve the complexities of a legendary man's character – it unfolds as a search for the meaning of his dying word, 'Rosebud' – but it is actually a piece of prestidigitation which makes the character disappear behind a flourish of artifice and mystery. At the end, the secret to Kane's personality is as hermetically sealed as the snowy image inside the glass ball which he drops, and shatters, when he dies at the beginning. Like *The War of the Worlds*, *Kane* has tended to overshadow its creator's subsequent achievements, those 'rougher' works which go beyond the tricks of theatre to a more intimate exploration of character. Welles was trying to make the Last Word in movies, looting Hollywood for its finest techniques and technicians to build himself an immortal monument. It is the scope of his youthful presumption which keeps *Kane* perpetually fresh and exciting.

Though there has been a surprising amount of pussyfooting around the subject, Kane's resemblance to William Randolph Hearst was obvious to most viewers when the film appeared, and a reading

of W. A. Swanberg's excellent *Citizen Hearst* will reveal the extent to which the film borrows from the life of 'the great yellow journalist'. Welles has confined himself to ironic comments – e.g. 'Some fine day, if Mr Hearst isn't frightfully careful, I'm going to make a film that's *really* based on his life' (1941) and 'Kane would have liked to see a film on his life, but not Hearst – he didn't have quite enough style' (1965). However, it seems that Hearst greatly enjoyed seeing his life dramatized on the screen. It is reported that he owned a print and showed it to his friends. The son of a former Hearst executive told me that at the yearly San Simeon conferences, the executives would greet Hearst with 'How's old Citizen Kane?' and he would get a big kick out of it.

Apparently Hearst's somewhat half-hearted approval of Louella Parsons's attacks on *Kane* was in deference to Marion Davies, who understandably was bothered by the unsparing depiction of Susan Alexander Kane and reportedly referred to the film as 'that g-g-g-goddam *Citizen Kane*'. Kane is of course an autonomous dramatic character, existing apart from any reference to Hearst, but there is value in noting where the characters of Kane and his prototype intersect, and where they diverge. Interestingly, it is where they diverge that the film most resembles autobiography. Hearst, for example, lived with his parents until he was nineteen and continued to see them, but Welles's mother died when he was eight – Kane's age when Thatcher takes him from Mary – and his father when he was thirteen. Again Welles shies from the comparison ('I had no Rosebuds'), but there are more points of contact than he will acknowledge.

There has also been a long-standing controversy over the authorship of *Kane's* script. It flared up recently when Pauline Kael published a long article in *The New Yorker* claiming that Herman J. Mankiewicz, who shared the screenplay credit with Welles, was in fact almost entirely responsible for the script from idea to final draft. Rather than interrupt this critical study with a detailed reply to her charges, I refer the interested reader to my article 'Rough Sledding with Pauline Kael' in the Fall 1971 *Film Heritage*. But for the record, a brief outline here. Miss Kael admitted to me that she had deliberately avoided talking to Welles or his partisans, so I asked Bogdanovich to give concrete evidence on Welles's side of the dispute. 'Kael's *Kane*,' he replied, 'is so studded with errors it'd be

Citizen Kane: staircase politics (Welles and Ray Collins)

impossible to fill you in quickly. I have a sworn statement, written at the time, from Richard Barr – associate producer on *Kane*, now a Broadway producer – which clearly explains how the project came into being. It was Orson's original idea – and Barr recounts how Welles wrote, rewrote, and changed the script as it went along. This affidavit – which Barr re-read a few weeks ago and again certified as 100% true – will appear in my book. Since Kael talked to Mankiewicz's secretary, I talked to Orson's, Miss Katherine Trosper. She said if Orson Welles didn't write a word of *Kane*, she wondered what all that dictation was which she took before and during production.'

John Houseman, who worked as Mankiewicz's editor during the scriptwriting, can hardly be described as a Welles partisan (Welles recently described him as 'an old enemy of mine'), but he said in 1969 that after he and Mankiewicz finished their work, 'Orson took over and visualised the script. He added a great deal of material himself, and later he and Herman had a dreadful row over the screen credit. As far as I could judge, the co-billing was correct. The *Citizen Kane* script was the product of both of them.' The ironic part of the controversy is that, in the end, it doesn't much matter what exact percentages of the script Welles and Mankiewicz wrote. Miss Kael herself acknowledges that the greatness of the film is in the direction: '*Kane* does something so well, and with such spirit, that the fulness and completeness of it continue to elate us. The formal elements themselves produce elation; we are kept aware of how marvellously worked out the ideas are.' The final version of the script is a model of screenwriting, for it doesn't attempt to direct the film on paper; it reads almost like a play, setting each scene briefly, with a few atmospheric suggestions, and following with dialogue and a minimum of technical notes. If it is true, as Houseman has said, that *Kane's* 'conception and structure were ... essentially Mankiewicz's', it is also true, he added, that 'Orson turned *Kane* into a film; the dynamics and the tensions are his, and the brilliant cinematic effects – all those visual and aural tensions that add up to make *Citizen Kane* one of the world's great movies – those were pure Orson Welles.'

Kane's death at the film's inception occurs in a fantastic, dreamlike context to which the audience has no orientation. The jump-cut from the death to the newsreel continues the disorientation. Though

Citizen Kane: after the newsreel. 'You've got to tell us *who he was.*'

the newsreel shows the events of Kane's life in their relation to historical time, placing Emily's death in 1918, his death in 1941, etc., it is only when we are shown the *News on the March* reporters conferring in the projection room that we are placed in a coherent time system. Now the film's present tense, the prosaic, anti-romantic aspect, is introduced. A system has been created in which all of Kane's actions are now in the past tense – and hence no longer of any effect. Welles's use of time counterpoints Kane's apparently powerful actions with the audience's foreknowledge that those actions will fail and that he will remain as he was shown at the beginning of the two hours: destroyed. The events of his life as we will see them exist in a limbo of moral futility.

When the newsreel ends, we see the beam throwing it to the screen, then hands turning off the projector, which halts with a whir. It is as if the movie world has been declared void, but only 'as if', for *Citizen Kane* continues. Welles wants to shock us out of our acceptance of the newsreel as truth about Kane, and wants further to shock us by showing a man, Rawlston, the newsreel editor, standing and waving his arms in the very light with which the newsreel has just been shown. Welles keeps Rawlston's face in shadow – as he does that of Thompson, the *auteur* of the newsreel, throughout the film – to emphasize the distance necessary to the artist's inquiry. We see Thompson and are thus able to 'identify' with his viewpoint, but we never see him completely, and are thus forced to temper our sympathy with irony. Kane's face is completely in shadow at his most selfless moment, when he reads the Declaration of Principles and signs it, pausing before he says 'Kane', and giving an odd hollowness to the word. The shifting reportorial attitudes of Kane, Leland, and Thompson form a running ironic motif about the possibility of presenting truth 'objectively'.

Rawlston tells Thompson, 'It isn't enough to tell us what a man did. You've got to tell us *who he was.*' Overriding Thompson's protests and the wisecracks of the other reporters, among whom, without make-up, are Joseph Cotten (Leland) and Erskine Sanford (the old *Inquirer* editor, Carter), Rawlston sends him out in quest of Rosebud: 'Maybe he told us all about himself on his deathbed.' To which another reporter calls out, 'Yeah, and maybe he didn't.' Cotten is heard muttering 'Rosebud' in a mocking tone of voice, just as he will do later as Leland at the end of Thompson's search; his presence here as a sort of Leland *doppelgänger* suggests that the search is doomed to failure – Thompson will be running around in circles. The reporter, who stands for the audience, also stands for the artist approaching the contradictions of his subject-matter. Intrigued, or rather forced, to speculate on the meaning of a word or an action, he goes in closer search of the possible implications of the clue. In the course of seeking further development of his preliminary image, he finds both support and negation of it, gradually modifying it and then abandoning his search just short of finding a definitive solution to the problem. The reporter goes as far as he can – within feet, in fact, of Rosebud – but he never does reach it. Welles and the audience do 'find' Rosebud, of course, but this, as we shall see, only demonstrates that Thompson was correct in accepting Kane's contradictions and not judging him.

'With me,' Welles said in a recent interview, 'the visual is a solution to what the poetic and musical form dictates. I don't begin with the visual and then try to find a poetry or music and try to stick it in the picture. The picture has to follow it. And again, people tend to think that my first preoccupation is with the simple plastic effects of the cinema. But to me they all come out of an interior rhythm, which is like the shape of music or the shape of poetry. I don't go around like a collector picking up beautiful images and pasting them together ... I believe in the film as a poetic medium. I don't think it competes with painting, or with ballet – the visual side of films is a key to poetry. There is no picture which justifies itself, no matter how beautiful, striking, horrific, tender ... it doesn't mean anything unless it makes poetry possible. And that suggests something, because poetry should make your hair stand up on your skin, should suggest things, evoke more than you see. The danger in the cinema is that you see everything, because it's a camera. So what you have to do is to manage to evoke, to incant, to raise up things which are not really there ... And the interior conception of the author, above all, must have a single shape.'

The rest of the film is coloured by what we have seen in the newsreel, the first statement we have received about Kane. The reporter's subsequent inquiries are for him and for us a kind of criticism of the magniloquent *News on the March*. (And of the documentary approach?) What we saw in the newsreel undoubtedly happened to Kane; he did live in the castle we are shown, did make the speeches we hear, etc. But the camera also lies ('there is no picture which justifies itself'), and we are not yet able to go beyond the surface to comprehend the 'interior rhythm', the poetry, of Kane's life. The image is suspect in *Kane*; each moment in the musical pattern of the film has its significance only in the context of all the other moments, past and to come. What is on the screen at a given moment is not definitive but is part of a state of mind shared by the author and his audience. Kane's actions are seen in two forms: in *précis* in the newsreel, more fully in the subsequent parts of the film. The tension of the structure is a fusion of suspense and mystery, a kind of metaphysical tension: suspense in that we (with Thompson) have foreknowledge of the actions we see Kane perform; mystery in that we are trying to discover the 'secret' behind them, Rosebud. Kane's life as we see it follows the scheme of classical tragedy, but it does not follow the *form* of classical tragedy. His end, in fact, comes at the very beginning of the film. We see his other actions out of order, through the reporter's eyes. The negation of the idea of Aristotelian chronology as it applies to Kane implies a deterministic suspension of the laws of cause and effect. The fugal

Citizen Kane: George Coulouris, Welles and Everett Sloane

structure of the film makes us see his life not as the strong, simple, straightforward action of classical tragedy but as a futile, cyclical 'theme and variations'.

Significantly, neither of Kane's closest friends, Leland and Bernstein, appears in the newsreel. The script called for them to be present in the shots of Kane's wedding to Emily, but Welles wisely omitted them. 'All I saw on that screen is that Charles Foster Kane is dead – I know that, I read the papers,' Rawlston jokingly comments. What we saw obviously is the product of a man who has no personal acquaintance with his subject. All Thompson has done is to read the papers and look at the newsreel footage. But for a brief section of 'bootlegged' footage of the elderly Kane being wheeled through his rose garden, the newsreel has shown us only what Kane did for the public's eye. (We even see him trying to smash the camera of an *Inquirer* photographer after his marriage to Susan!) The inclusion of the bootlegged footage, like the one sequence in Hitchcock's *Rear Window* shot outside of the hero's perspective, helps to ensure our awareness of the perceptual strategy involved. A title in the newsreel fills the screen with the paradoxically true and false words, 'Few private lives were more public.'

Thompson's search is a chronological, Aristotelian drama. He changes during the beginning-to-end frame of the film, a period of something more than a week from Kane's death to the end of his research into Kane's life. The climax of Thompson's drama comes when he tells the elderly Bernstein that Leland has 'nothing particular the matter with him, they tell me, just . . .' and makes an embarrassed pause. Bernstein finishes the sentence for him: 'Just old age,' and adds, 'It's the only disease, Mr Thompson, that you don't look forward to being cured of.' Thereafter Thompson is less and less detached, and finally he is repelled by the callousness shown by Kane's butler. He is seeing himself as he had been at the beginning of the search. Like Leland, like Kane himself, Thompson is an innocent cruelly brought to recognize corruption. The sobering effect of age is constantly brought home in the juxtapositions of the young and old Kane, the young and old Leland, the young Thompson and the old Bernstein and Leland.

The counterpoint between Thompson's dramatic growth and Kane's futile attempts to change the course of his life contributes subconsciously to the irony of the film, just as the absolute symmetry of the film's construction maintains a constant ironic counterpoint to the utter lack of order in Kane's life. To give just one example of the hundreds of symmetrical devices, the photograph of Kane, Emily, and their son used in the paper when the mother and son die in an automobile accident appears in the newsreel immediately after Kane and Emily strike a pose for their wedding picture. Then, much later, we see the actual taking of the photograph – at the moment before Emily sends the boy home in the car and tells Kane that they are going to Susan's apartment: where Kane will decide to end the marriage. It takes dozens of viewings to become fully conscious of this kind of subliminal metaphor, though one does sense its operation. We feel what Gertrude Stein called 'the pleasure of concentrating on the final simplicity of excessive complication.'

In the doggedness of Thompson's search and in its final futility, Welles is mocking the audience's hope for a pat solution to Kane's life. Leland mocks it: 'Rosebud? Yeah, I saw that in *The Inquirer*. Well, I never believed anything I saw in *The Inquirer*. Anything else?' Thompson alone of the reporters who gather in Xanadu at the end realizes that there is, finally, no solution. Someone tells him that if he had found out what Rosebud meant, it would have explained everything. Facing the camera, though still in shadow and with the camera receding from him, he says, 'No, I don't think so. No. Mr Kane was a man who got everything he wanted and then lost it. Maybe Rosebud was something he couldn't get or something he lost, but anyway it wouldn't have *explained* anything. No, I guess Rosebud is just a piece in a jigsaw puzzle – a missing piece.'

Then the missing piece is filled in, but what may we make of the completed puzzle? Welles's camera leaves Thompson for majestic tracking shots over the vast pile of objects Kane has spent his life in accumulating ... among them a headless statue of Venus, linked in an earlier camera movement with his mother's stove. From the high shots of the pile, we move in to a privileged shot: Rosebud, Kane's childhood sled, filling the screen, burning. Dwight Macdonald is a typical viewer in stating that he gets 'a big thrill' out of this shot, though he can't explain why. With the shot we see the 'solution' for which we and Thompson have been searching, and we realize that it does in fact solve nothing. Thompson is dignified by our realization that we had to see Rosebud to reach his understanding.

But is it possible, as some viewers feel, that the reporter's speech is ironic, that seeing the emotionally potent image of the burning sled makes us realize that there *is* an explanation? Hardly, for the revelation of Rosebud, far from explaining the mystery of Kane's futile existence, adds another dimension to it. If Welles had not shown us Rosebud, we would have continued to think that there could be a solution, and that Thompson is merely unable to find it. We would be left to conjure up our own solutions. Instead, by recalling Kane's expulsion from his childhood home and his use of the sled as a weapon against Thatcher, Welles is completing the cycle of Kane's life by going back to the starting-point – to the moment when he still had a chance. Despite the suggestions of a Lost Eden in the scene of Kane's expulsion from his home (the snow, the long unbroken tracking shot, the huge caressing close-up of mother and child), it is important to remember that Kane's childhood was far from idyllic.

When we first see the child, vignetted through a window in the distance, he is playing by himself in the snow, as solitary and helpless as in his old age. The family tensions are sketched in quickly

Citizen Kane: 'Why is she sending Charles away?' (Agnes Moorehead, George Coulouris, Harry Shannon)

and cryptically: the mother is domineering but anguished as she commits her son to Thatcher; the father is pathetic and clumsy in his objections. Why is she sending Charles away? To get him away from his father, who apparently abuses the boy when drunk? Perhaps. But more likely, given the aura of helplessness with which Welles surrounds the entire family, it is simply that the accident which made the Kanes suddenly rich (a defaulting boarder left them stock in a booming silver mine) has created its own fateful logic – Charles must 'get ahead'. What gives the brief leave-taking scene its mystery and poignancy is precisely this feeling of predetermination. The sled with which little Kane blindly and instinctively lashes out at his fate becomes a symbol not of what his life was but what it could have been. The journey away from home is evoked in a haunting shot of the sled lying half buried in the snow as a mournful train whistle blows on the soundtrack.

When the elderly Kane clutches the glass ball and murmurs 'Rosebud,' it is at the moment when Susan (who reminded him of his mother) leaves him. An astonishing and all but invisible touch connects the childhood scene with the beginning of Kane's affair with Susan. When Mrs Kane sits down at the table to sign the papers giving Charles to Thatcher, the camera makes an infinitesimal pan to the right, revealing in the background, on a table, the glass ball. Years later, in Susan's apartment, the ball appears again, hidden among a clutter of bric-à-brac on a table, with the magical illogic of a poetic metaphor. When Susan leaves Xanadu, Kane discovers the ball among Susan's belongings, and it will be with him on his deathbed. What makes Kane's last word and the image of the sled so powerful is this entire undercurrent of suggestions – suggestions which point at something illusory, unattained, and perhaps unattainable.

Though the author himself is prone to apologize for Rosebud – 'It's a gimmick, really, and rather dollar-book Freud' – we should trust the tale, not the teller, and consider also the shots following those of the burning sled: smoke rising from the castle and dissolving into the dark sky, a dissolve to our initial position behind the 'No Trespassing' sign, and then a dissolve to Xanadu seen again from behind the giant 'K', altered now by the darkness of the window behind which Kane died, dawn light faintly shining on the clouds around the castle, and the smoke rising from above it. The repetition of two perspectives from the enigmatic opening sequence (which the script describes as 'Ankor Wat, the night the last King died') forces us to acknowledge that although Kane's dilemma has been illuminated, the evidence is still open to consideration, and the mystery remains. As Robin Wood observed of the psychiatrist's explanation of Norman Bates at the end of *Psycho*: 'The psychiatrist, glib and complacent, reassures us. But Hitchcock crystallizes this for us merely to force us to reject it. We shall see on reflection that the "explanation" ignores as much as it explains.' Hitchcock then shows us Norman, whom we 'understand', sitting wrapped in a womb-like blanket, irretrievably irrational; and then the car withdrawing from the swamp. Similarly, the last sequence of *Kane*, under which merge the two counterpointed motives of the musical score – the 'power' motif in brass and the 'Rosebud' motif on the vibraphone, as composer Bernard Herrmann described them – resolves the situation into perfect ambiguity.

Thompson's cockiness has been supplanted with humility. He now has an empathy with Kane which was only perfunctorily expressed in *News on the March*. By vicariously experiencing the events he represented in his newsreel, he has come to understand that Kane was more than 'an emperor of newsprint'. In a speech included in the final version of the script but not in the film, Thompson has this to say to a reporter who asks him what he has discovered: 'Well – it's become a very clear picture. He was the most honest man who ever lived, with a streak of crookedness a yard wide. He was a liberal and a reactionary. He was a loving husband – and both his wives left him. He had a gift for friendship such as few men have – and he broke his oldest friend's heart like you'd throw away a cigarette you were through with. Outside of that —' This is best out of the film, since it merely puts into words what is so powerfully made felt through the sight and sound of the ending scenes. But it is a hint of the film's method, the constant ironic undercutting of the audience's search for a solution.

The title itself expresses the central paradox. 'Citizenship,' alliance with effective human society, is the goal to which Kane/Cain vainly aspires. He speaks the word 'citizens' twice, at the times in which his purest societal impulses are manifested, but moments also of the highest irony: when he is reading the Declaration of Principles – 'I will also provide them with a fighting and tireless champion of their rights as citizens, and as human beings' – and when he is delivering his campaign speech to the 'decent, ordinary citizens'. Welles undercuts the spirit of Kane's high-minded speech by cutting to the dandyish Leland on the words 'the working man and the slum child' and to Bernstein and his unsavoury associates applauding after the words 'the under-privileged, the underpaid, and the underfed'.

Citizen represents the heroic, effective aspect of Kane; *Kane* represents his foredoomed, predetermined aspect. Our heroic conception of Kane as a tragically flawed character marching through time to his doom is tempered with an understanding that he was not in complete control of the events of his life, that some force has ordered them. Thompson's presence further emphasizes this tension, as do Gregg Toland's use of deep-focus photography, the recurrence of low-angle shots, and the virtual absence of close-ups, all strategies which tend to integrate the character into the milieu. The most explicit expression of determinism in the film comes when Susan leaves Kane. The screeching cockatoo flies past

Citizen Kane: Susan in Xanadu (Dorothy Comingore)

the camera, and we see Kane standing in shock at the door of her room in the extreme background. In medium shot, he pivots mechanically back into the room, and Welles cuts to a low-angled shot of the rest of the motion; Kane moves like a marionette, a feeling intensified by the formalizing device of changing the angle of a continuous motion. The lowness of the angle abstracts him into a shape, non-rational, a phenomenon of milieu.

Given the example of the newsreel, it might be assumed that the events of Kane's life included in each of the other narrators' flashbacks – the Thatcher manuscript and the recollections of Bernstein, Leland, Susan, and Raymond – are grouped together not by chance but for metaphorical reasons. Such is the case. Thatcher's section has to do entirely with power plays: his taking Charles away from his parents, his giving Kane a substitute sled, Kane's retaliation by means of his newspaper, and finally Thatcher's taking of the newspaper from Kane and Kane telling him, 'I always gagged on that silver spoon.'

Bernstein is childlike. His flashback shows an idealized Kane and

◀ *Citizen Kane:* 'It was a marriage just like any other marriage.' Shots from the breakfast montage

Citizen Kane: Susan's attempted suicide

contains most of the triumphal moments of Kane's career. Of all the characters in the film, Bernstein remains the best-disposed towards Kane, who demanded nothing from him but camaraderie. The placement of events in Bernstein's section also equates him with the beginnings of Kane's newspaper and political careers . . . the days when he was conquering the world. Bernstein and the more sceptical Leland are repeatedly seen facing each other in profile across the frame, and their radical opposition dramatizes the difference between the emotional demands they make on Kane. The last time the two are together, on the night of the disastrous opera, Bernstein faces Leland and tells him in a strange and moving tone, 'I guess that'll show you.' As the script indicates, the line is delivered 'with a kind of quiet passion, rather than triumph'.

If the selfless Bernstein is equated with loyalty, Leland, the romantic idealist, is equated with love. In his flashback, we see all the phases of Kane's love life, from the idyllic beginning of marriage to the meeting with Susan, the confrontation with Gettys in Susan's apartment, the resultant rupture from Emily and from Leland himself, the marriage to the 'singer', and finally Susan's and Kane's humiliations in the opera and Kane's reading of Leland's review with a hollow laugh which sounds more like a sob. Since he is a romantic, Leland feels and remembers all of the emotional extremes which the other characters are prone to remember only selectively. In Bernstein's flashback, for example, we see Emily only in awe-stricken long-shot, but in Leland's we see the marriage dissolving from tenderness to coldness, in the breakfast montage; Susan's flashback shows only the catastrophic moments of her relationship with Kane, but Leland's shows the catastrophe and the courtship. Time and again, Welles emphasizes Leland's brooding presence in showing the progress of Kane's love life. His face is held in a lap dissolve over the start of the breakfast montage, and again over the end of the montage. 'It was a marriage just like any other marriage,' is his melancholy comment. Again, when he tells about Kane meeting Susan, his face is held for several seconds over the rainy street. Finally, when Leland walks away from Thompson between the arms of two callous nurses, there occurs the most profound device of the film: he vanishes into the billboard picture of Susan.

In Leland's first scene with Thompson at the hospital, the script calls for the camera to move, after a few lines, from Thompson's face to Leland's, but Welles had decided to keep the reporter's face constantly out of direct sight of the camera. So we share Thompson's obsessive stare at Leland. Welles's transposition of the lines, 'I can remember absolutely everything, young man, that's my curse. That's the greatest curse ever inflicted on the human race, memory,' from a position later in the speech to the very opening of the scene has an important effect on our view of Leland – as an embodiment of Kane's past, the physical presence of his memory, a living Rosebud, the better part of his nature. Seen in this perspective, Leland's action in refusing to answer Kane's letter from Xanadu is the last refusal of Kane's conscience to accept his gesture of reconciliation. Leland's monologue is Joycean in its tragicomic caesuras (from '. . . We do believe in *something*' to 'You're absolutely *sure* you haven't got a cigar?'); all the more so in the lines as Cotten speaks them.

Leland is never seen with a woman, though there is a hint of an infatuation with Emily: 'I can tell you about Emily. I went to dancing school with Emily. I was very graceful. – We were talking about the first Mrs Kane.' The script did in fact contain a scene (in a brothel) in which Kane tries unsuccessfully to interest Leland in a girl. He ignores her and challenges Kane about dragging the country into war. Leland personifies Kane's loving impulses, and his flaw is candour. He tells Kane what he thinks about Susan, and is punished, like Cordelia in *King Lear*, like Falstaff, for loving too freely and simply. Kane tells lies, overreaches, creates a myth about himself, and finally crushes the *alter ego* who questions the human effect of that power. Leland's presence emphasizes the limits of Kane's ability to love. He plays Abel to Kane.

5: The Magnificent Ambersons

'Showmanship in place of genius: a new deal at RKO.'
Trade advertisement, 1942

Welles's boyhood resembled Kane's, but in many ways George Orson Welles was closer to George Amberson Minafer. Bred in genteel Midland towns, the boys were exceptional, George Minafer as the last of the aristocrats, Welles as an intellectual outsider. Welles's father, like Eugene Morgan in *The Ambersons*, was an inventor. His works included the U.S. Army mess kit, a steam-driven aeroplane, and a carbide bicycle lamp; the last of the Amberson fortune is squandered on automobile headlights. 'At the turn of the century,' Welles recalls, 'my father began making bicycle lamps because he thought there was no future in the automotive business. He made a fortune in spite of himself, inasmuch as the automobile manufacturers bought the lamps for their cars.' The doomed romance between Eugene and Isabel Amberson, and the subsequent orphaning of her son, strongly reflects Welles's own childhood.

George Minafer is Charlie Kane given a decade's reprieve. Kane's snow scene is brief, tense, claustrophobic, punctuated by small, sharp camera movements. His childhood is over in minutes. George's Eden lasts years longer, and his expulsion is delayed for thirty minutes on the screen. The camera movements in his film are longer, more graceful, his snow scene more relaxed. George's innocence ends with a long iris-in, a tribute both to the passing of an age – the death of his father and the birth of the automobile – and to the conventions of an earlier, more graceful age of movies. As *Chimes at Midnight* is a lament for the *conception* of Merrie England, *The Ambersons*, Welles has said, is a lament 'not so much for the epoch as for the sense of moral values which are destroyed.'

After *Citizen Kane* Welles wanted to make *The Pickwick Papers* with W. C. Fields, but that Falstaff was already under contract to make the film with another studio. RKO still considered Welles's long-standing *Heart of Darkness* project too experimental, and he finally decided to write a script based on Booth Tarkington's novel, which had won a Pulitzer Prize in 1919 but had been almost forgotten in the interim. It had been filmed once before, as *Pampered Youth*, a 1925 silent directed by David Smith. Ben Alexander played George as a boy, and Cullen Landis was George as a young man.

Welles had adapted *Penrod* and *Seventeen* for his *First Person Singular* series of narrated radio shows – Tarkington was one of his favourite authors – and on 29 October 1939 had presented his adaptation of *The Ambersons*, starring himself and Walter Huston. When he came to make the film, in late 1941, he took exceptional care with its soundtrack. Robert Wise, who edited Welles's first two features, recalls that Welles was nervous about recording some loops needed for post-synchronization on *Kane*. After the looping was done, however, he was so taken with the process that he decided to make a pre-production recording of the dialogue for *The Ambersons* and have the actors synchronize their lips and motions to it. The first day of shooting was a fiasco: the actors could hardly act, let alone synchronize. Wise says that everyone but Welles and the actors found the whole matter hilarious, and it was abandoned by lunchtime.

Unsuccessful though it was, the experiment in 'radio sound' furthered Welles's work. Howard Hawks had developed rapid-fire overlapping dialogue, notably in *His Girl Friday* (1940), and Alfred Hitchcock had experimented with aural montage as early as *Blackmail* (1929). Few directors besides Welles and Hitchcock, however, have exploited what Welles's (and later Hitchcock's) composer, Bernard Herrmann, called 'radio scoring' in a 1941 New York *Times* article. Herrmann explains that these are 'musical cues which last only a few seconds . . . in radio drama, every scene must be bridged by some sort of sound device, so that even five seconds of music becomes a vital instrument in telling the ear that the scene is shifting.' Herrmann conceived of some scenes in *Kane*, such as the breakfast montage, as 'ballet suites', and Welles cut them to match the music. Herrmann worked closely with Welles on new uses of sound effects and orchestration, and in *The Ambersons* the two

The Magnificent Ambersons: the ball at the Amberson mansion

carried their experiments to a new degree. Ten and twenty-minute sections are almost continuously underscored with music, and over-lapping dialogue is made to serve new dramatic functions.

Welles wrote the script of *The Ambersons* in nine days, no doubt helped by his radio experience with the book. Shooting began on 28 October 1941. At night he was acting in Norman Foster's *Journey Into Fear*, a Mercury production for which he directed several scenes and helped Joseph Cotten write the script. On Sundays he was recording radio shows for the 'Lady Esther' series; and all this pressure, added to the studio's increasing uneasiness over *Kane's* distribution problems, forced him to let Wise and several other associates direct two short scenes. Shooting was completed on 22 January, and Welles left for South America on 4 February to shoot *It's All True*, his abortive documentary. He took along a rough cut of *The Ambersons* and edited it in long-distance conversations with Wise.

In the spring of 1942, RKO gave the film a sneak preview. At this stage it was a hundred and thirty-one minutes long. The audience found it slow and unintentionally comic; since Welles was away, Wise and Welles's manager, Jack Moss, were ordered to make cuts. A second preview was not a success, so further cuts were made, Welles's ending was scrapped, a new ending was shot, other scenes were redone, and the last two reels were wholly reshuffled. The third sneak convinced the studio to release *The Ambersons* – now down to its present length of eighty-eight minutes – and it was double-billed with a Lupe Velez film.

In the meantime RKO had undergone a change in hierarchy, and one of the new studio head Charles Koerner's first moves was to order Welles to return from Brazil, bringing shooting on *It's All True* to an end, and strip him of his contract and the *It's All True* footage, to which he was denied access. His Mercury staff were given twenty-four hours to vacate their offices, ostensibly to make room for a unit producing a Tarzan picture. *Journey Into Fear* was edited without Welles's approval. He threatened to sue but agreed to shoot a new ending for it and to recut the last reel. He even narrated a short *gratis* for the privilege, but was furious with everyone involved in the 'mutilation' of *The Ambersons* and remained so for years. He said that 'they let the studio janitor cut *The Magnificent Ambersons* in my absence'. He claimed also that the studio had failed to give the film adequate advance publicity on the grounds that it was an irredeemable flop. Today he explains that 'about forty-five minutes were cut out – the whole heart of the picture really – for which the first part had been a preparation . . . The film has a silly ending . . . just ridiculous . . . It bears no relation to my script.'

RKO's advertising tried to mask the sombreness of the story with sensationalism – 'Scandal played no favourites when that high-and-mighty Amberson girl fell in love once too often!' read the New York ad on the day of the première. The film was not a success with the public nor with most of the reviewers, James Agee in *Time* being an exception, and is only today beginning to be appreciated for the great – though flawed – work that it is. Like *Greed* and *Que Viva Mexico!*, it represents only part of its director's conception.

The transitions perhaps are what strike one most about *Citizen Kane*, but what one remembers from *The Ambersons* is the fluidity of each scene. The transitions in *Kane* draw attention to themselves and are the basis for the film's cyclical narrative structure; *The Ambersons* disguises its cuts and uses long sensuous dissolves to emphasize the inevitability, the flow, of the story's linear progression. This impressed François Truffaut, who wrote that 'there are surely fewer than two hundred shots in this story which covers twenty-five years.' Actually there are a great many more than that, but the fact that such a sophisticated viewer was deceived indicates the effectiveness of Welles's strategy.

For the effect of *The Ambersons* lies largely in the quiet frustration of the audience. Welles holds each shot a little longer than is normal; thirty seconds or a minute (or longer) is such an uncommon length for a shot that we are unconsciously drawn into thinking that it will last still longer. And when Welles does cut, for the most part unobtrusively, there is a slight disappointment – a nostalgia – that the scene is already over. To achieve this requires high concentration in each shot. The overlapping conversations, the continuous use of music, and the flowing motion of and before the camera achieve the grace and intensity needed for the effect. The fact that the collapse of a family and the deterioration of a town takes only an hour and a half and yet is so convincingly real is the final triumph of the film, which, unlike other films of 'grow old and die' novels, does not satisfy itself with indicating nostalgia but actually creates it.

D. W. Griffith's *True Heart Susie* and Jean Renoir's *Une Partie de Campagne* have this effect, as does Truffaut's *Jules et Jim*, which starts the year *The Ambersons* ends, 1912, and shows clearly its debt to all three films. The structure of Truffaut's film, as he admits, weakens in the last sections, as does that of *The Ambersons* for reasons not entirely due to the studio's recutting. To create a mood so buoyant as that achieved in the first half-hour of each film and let it down gracefully into destruction proved too taxing for both young directors. And, as might be expected, Truffaut's comment on the style of *The Ambersons* is precisely correct: 'This film was made in violent contrast to *Citizen Kane*, almost as if by another film-maker who detested the first and wanted to give him a lesson in modesty.'

The frame is edged with soft-focus in the early shots, which have the feeling of old photographs coming magically to life. Manny Farber complained that the first shots are no more than a succession of 'postcards' connected by narration, but the flow of the section depends on this kind of time-compressing exposition, disguised by the soft, whimsical music (including a jaunty ragtime adaptation of a theme from Verdi's *La Traviata*, another story of ill-fated love) and by Welles's skilful narration. Seen silently it would have less connection, but with the soundtrack, the streetcar, the men in the bar, the rowboat, the stovepipe hat, and Eugene modelling clothes go by in smooth and natural succession. The extreme economy of this sequence is part of its beauty. The novel has a similar beginning – wry comments on the mores of the 1870s – but takes three chapters to get through George's childhood years. Given the advantage of being able to *show* the period evolving, Welles compresses George's first seventeen years into less than ten minutes. 'The magnificence of the Ambersons began in 1873. Their splendour lasted throughout all the years that saw their Midland town spread and darken into a city . . .' In the first two sentences of narration, Welles summarizes the rise and eventual collapse of the Amberson dynasty. The use in early scenes of the townspeople as a chorus and the designation of an old gossip as a 'prophetess' could hardly make the parallel with Greek tragedy more explicit; nor could the story's debt to *Oedipus Rex*, its tragic mother-son relationship, be more clear. By its very indirection, the poetic beginning heightens the tragedy that is to follow. What is left unsaid and what is treated playfully in the prologue to *The Ambersons* will echo throughout the slowly darkening remainder of the film.

Young George's two rapid rides through the town in his pony cart at ages nine and seventeen, separated by four short scenes, are perfect epitomizations of the later behaviour of 'Rides-Down-Everything', Lucy Morgan's name for him. Welles tells us that 'George Amberson Minafer, the Major's one grandson, was a princely terror', as we see his cart gradually approaching the camera in extreme long shot. As he drives out of the frame left, Welles cuts to him driving left through a labourer's sand pile, then shows him driving away from the camera and through the town in three more shots. 'There were people – grown people they were,' the narration continues, 'who expressed themselves longingly – they did hope to see the day, they said, when that boy would get his comeuppance.'

As he did with Rosebud several times in the early parts of *Kane*, Welles mocks his own central motif. He cuts to a couple on the street: 'His *what*?' asks the lady. 'His come*up*pance,' answers the gentleman in his most determined tones. 'Something's bound to take him down some day; I only want to *be* there.' This is one of the first indications of the slight variation in attitude between the novel and the film: Welles's distance from the characters is slightly greater than Tarkington's, a fact which no doubt accounts for much of the tittering of audiences unable to see the satire. When Eugene falls through the bass viol early in the film, Welles is telling how the instruments of the serenade will 'presently release their melodies to the dulcet stars'. Tarkington used the line with softer irony in referring to the popular songs of the day.

The second ride through the town is down from six shots to four, and the speed of the carriage is greatly increased: the cutting is more rapid, smaller portions of the right-to-left arc are used, and the effect is that George has indeed returned from college 'with the same stuffing'. The third shot, just after George has snapped his whip at another labourer, pans from ground level right with the carriage. The spinning hub veers close to the camera in a succinct visual metaphor for George's *hubris*.

Welles's Hollywood enemies attributed the success of *Kane* to Gregg Toland, the great photographer who worked closely with him in planning the shots and the texture of the film. By the time *The Ambersons* went on the floor, Toland was working with John Ford in the Navy's combat photography unit. Stanley Cortez furthered Toland's work with deep-focus, which is used in almost all of *The Ambersons*' shots. André Bazin has dealt at length with the psychological and dialectical advantages of giving equal focal stress to each object in a scene (with Toland's processes, objects 200 feet from the camera are as sharp as those in the extreme foreground). The director can choreograph his scenes with great subtlety, changing the audience's viewpoint without the intervention of a cut. Bazin found that the deep-focus work of Jean Renoir, and of Toland for William Wyler and Welles, represented a revolution in film style, an assertion of the integrality of space and time in direct opposition to the classical theories of montage.

Toland stated simply that it obviated the 'loss of realism' due to breaking a scene up into 'long and short angles'. Welles has stressed the gain in ambiguity: 'The public may choose, with its eyes, what it wants to see of a shot. I don't like to force it.' The recurrent use of low angles, though seldom as deliberately obtrusive as in *Kane*, places further emphasis on the characters' relation to their surroundings. Cortez also achieved a chiaroscuro reminiscent of period daguerrotypes and of Billy Bitzer's photography for Griffith. The counterpoint between the almost documentary immediacy of the exteriors of *The Ambersons* (in itself a kind of stylization) and the meticulous stylization of the camera movement, action, and dialogue contributes much of the film's power. As James Agee perceptively remarked, the film is shot 'from a viewpoint so fresh that it creates a visual suspense in the very act of clarification'.

The predominance of the city and the baroque furnishings of the mansion, and the implicit family-mansion metaphor, impart a strong determinism to the story. George could hardly have helped growing up that way ('They-Couldn't-Help-It' is Lucy's name for the woods inhabited by Chief 'Rides-Down-Everything'). Welles's meticulous use of settings – the idyllic snowy fields with only telephone wires intruding, the somnolent little town providing a backdrop for George and Lucy's carriage ride, and the bustling, noisy city they later walk through (and the dirty metropolis George walks through alone) – all this carries the story of the town along with the story of the family. The film has epic quality, though it has been lessened by the recutting.

On George's return home, Welles tells us, 'cards were out for a ball in his honour, and this' – slight ironic pause – 'pageant of the tenantry was the last of the great, long-remembered dances that "everybody talked about".' The ball sequence lasts about ten minutes and is one of the most exhilarating moments in the history of the movies. After a distant shot of the mansion lit up for the ball, a slow dissolve reveals Eugene and Lucy, seen from behind, entering the house. The camera follows. The physical feeling in this shot is extraordinary: servants open the doors on either side, pulling hard against the wind and smiling broadly as they do it; Sam the butler bows and takes Eugene's hat; couples pass in front of the camera while in the background the party is in full gaiety (the camera all the time tracking in). And what to say of the other aspects of the scene – the sparkling, gently swaying cut-glass chandelier, the vines and flowers set all around the hall, the dazzling gowns of the women, the opulent coats and ties of the men.

A cut to an opposite viewpoint starts a slow tracking shot towards George and Isabel's receiving line. A lavishly decorated Christmas tree sweeps by on the left as the camera approaches Uncle John Minafer, a loud bumpkin telling the Major how he'll be laid out in this very hall 'when his time comes', and telling George, 'There was a time though in your fourth month when you was so puny nobody thought you'd live.' This line is tossed off, but in it lies a key to George's megalomania, an explanation of the absurd affection Isabel will lavish on him until her death. On her deathbed she will ask George if he has had enough to eat and if he has caught a cold on the trip home. One is reminded of the first words of Mrs Kane: 'Be careful, Charles! Pull your muffler around your neck, Charles!' As she says the words Charles reflexively does pull his muffler around his neck. George's reaction to his uncle's untactful line here, however, is a fierce, 'M'mber you v'ry well indeed!' The first real glimpse of George as a young man gives him away. His arch, elegant profile is set against the left of the frame as the camera stops tracking, and his face shows the ridiculous arrogance that is to doom his mother.

Eugene is now greeting Isabel, and Welles cuts to a shot of the three faces: George's wary on the left, Isabel's smiling, Eugene's in profile on the right. Immediately, wordlessly, the tension is established. When Eugene tells George that 'from now on you're going to see a lot of me – I hope', the violins off-camera start a gay tune. When Isabel introduces George to Lucy a few seconds later, the musicians are in the midst of a transition which becomes a high, plaintive note the moment after Isabel says, 'George, you don't remember her either, though of course you *will*.' Robert Rossen remarked on Welles's ability to tell an entire story in a single shot; here Herrmann tells an entire story with a bar of music.

The rest of the scene is increasingly fluid: a long track back with George and Lucy through the ballroom which cranes up with them as they walk up the stairs (and shows a violinist in the foreground playing the plaintive tune), a dissolve to a tracking shot of Lucy's suitors criss-crossing in front of George and the camera, a cut to George and Lucy seating themselves on the stairs, a soft-focus wipe to the family gathered around a punch bowl. This begins a shot which was to have been an unbroken revolution almost entirely around the dance floor.

After the Major teases Eugene and Isabel about the bass viol, the camera tracks slightly back, panning right and then left as George and Lucy walk past the refreshment table. As they walk away from it a middle-aged couple approach, and at this point several lines of dialogue about the town's latest delicacy – olives – were cut. 'Don't ask me why they wanted it out,' Welles says. 'The result was a useless jump in an otherwise unbroken scene.'

As it stands, the camerawork is dazzling enough – a cut replaces the intended pan left from the couple to Eugene and Isabel dancing, but the camera still seems to dance away with them, stand still for George and Lucy's brief conversation, and then retreat as the two dance away on the wonderful exchange about George's ambition: to be a yachtsman. Chances are that the olive remarks caused guffaws at the preview, partially because it is here that Welles's satire of his characters is most apparent. In the script, the couple's debate over the value of the delicacy goes thus: '... You're supposed to *eat* 'em ... I hear you gotta eat nine, and then you get to like them ... Well, I reckon most everybody'll be makin' a stagger to worm through nine of 'em, now Amberson's brought 'em to town.'

The ball ends more quickly than we would like (the best example of Welles's strategy of frustration), on a slow Sternbergian dissolve from Eugene and Isabel dancing in the foreground to them dancing in the extreme background after the rest of the dancers have gone. Here Welles's use of sound perspective is at its height. We hear, distantly, George and Lucy talking, then on a cut we hear them at normal volume; the music stops, in the foreground Eugene thanks Isabel, and from the audience's side of the camera we hear Jack: 'Bravo! Bravissimo!' Again we hear Eugene, then Lucy and George in the background. This linear use of three sound perspectives creates a remarkable illusion of depth, and the mingling of voices in the subsequent leave-takings heightens the scene's breathless tension. The choreography is similarly punctuated: Jack walks towards George, the camera panning left; Fanny runs in back of them; Isabel dashes in front of the camera. As the scene ends, Isabel is poised in the foreground between facing profiles of Lucy and George. The 'flat' screen becomes surreally three-dimensioned.

Shortly after this, in the family argument in the hall, Welles uses sound montage for another kind of super-real tension as Fanny's, Jack's, and George's voices follow each other in rapid irritated succession. Agnes Moorehead establishes Aunt Fanny's character as swiftly as she did Mrs Kane's. The idiotic laughter that greets Aunt Fanny at almost every showing of the film is an indication of how much of this tortured woman she compels the audience to see. It is a beautiful and frightening performance, and it moves me greatly each time I see the film.

The snow scene which follows offers a humorous contrast

The Magnificent Ambersons: the end of the ball ▶

The Magnificent Ambersons: George and Lucy in the snow (Tim Holt, Anne Baxter)

between the grace of the sleigh (which soon capsizes) and the grotesque rumblings of Eugene Morgan's 'broken-down chafing-dish'. The scenes of Morgan starting the car with George's reluctant assistance are played out against a stylized backdrop which includes houses, fences, and telephone wires. The automobile is still a diversion in this scene enacted in the purity of the snow – in one of the cut scenes George argues that people don't take their elephants visiting with them, so why should they take their automobiles? – and the riding song epitomizes the spirit of the scene as well as did 'Oh, Mr Kane!', which also marked the end of a carefree era. The novel had the riders singing 'The Star-Spangled Banner', but Welles mercifully lifted a song from a later chapter:

> As I walk along the Boy de Balong
>   With an independent air,
>   The people all declare,
>   'He must be a millionaire.'
> *Oh,* you hear them sigh, and wish to die,
>   And see them wink the other eye
> At the man who broke the bank at Monte Carlo!

The slow iris-in begins as the car and the singing diminish into the distance. The script has the film opening with an iris-out and the snow scene closing with a simple fade: the shifting was an inspired idea.

The *allegro* movement is over, and the gradual darkening begins. With a fade-in we see the mansion doors (which had opened on the ball scene shortly before), but now there is a wreath on one and Eugene's shadow on the other. The music stops abruptly as the door clicks shut behind the Morgans – indoors the neighbours and relatives are filing around a coffin. Placing the camera in the coffin's position was done notably by Carl Dreyer in *Vampyr* (1931), but of course for a different effect. Here it serves to nullify our feelings – if any, since we have hardly seen him – for Wilbur Minafer, George's father, with whom, in Truffaut's theory about the subjective and objective uses of the camera, it is now impossible to identify.

A film in which the camera actually plays a character, as in Welles's Conrad script or in Robert Montgomery's *The Lady in the Lake*, is the exact opposite of the subjective film, which depends on the audience identifying with the feelings of a character. And the only way to identify with a character, Truffaut concludes, is to see him. A classic example of the subjective camera is the little boy's interview with the psychiatrist in Truffaut's *Les Quatre Cents Coups*: the camera holds on the boy's face for the whole interview, and we see his feelings. Welles takes this basic filmic rule and makes it part of his own style. When the young Kane receives a Christmas sled from his guardian, for example, the camera tilts from his face to a grotesquely angled view of the towering Thatcher. In the same shot we see Charles and see Thatcher from the boy's angle – feeling as well the guardian's power over the boy.

Our attention is not on Wilbur in his coffin but on the family around it, and particularly on Fanny, who moves towards the camera and is then shown in great close-up, her face streaked with tears, more for herself than for her brother. A pointed little chorus follows on a dissolve from Fanny's face: two grim townsmen, staring into the camera as the mourners had done in the previous scene, one of them saying, 'Wilbur Minafer – quiet man – town'll hardly know he's gone.' The scene of the two men staring into the camera, taken from a low angle (grave's-eye view) and showing the men in formal (funeral) dress against a daytime sky, is not in the script. It was meant to follow a missing shot of Wilbur's gravestone.

The famous kitchen scene is the next retained in the released film. Welles seats the audience across from George as he stuffs himself, Fanny prodding him about Eugene's involvement with Isabel at his commencement, from which he has just returned. The camera makes two slight pans, one at the beginning and one at the end of the scene, and the effect is of eavesdropping on a confusing and revelatory confrontation between a person masking her emotions and another oblivious to them. We share each hesitation and gesture with the characters, prodded by no editorial device. The implication involved in showing the scene to us in its totality is that the hesitations are just as important as the gestures. The *mise-en-scène* is highly baroque: a clutter of pots hanging in the background, a giant stove in the left rear, long black shadows across the ceiling, a clutter of serving dishes, pitchers, and plates in the foreground. George stuffs himself relentlessly.

Welles has given an erroneous impression of this scene: 'The actors were rehearsed for five weeks before we started the film. And on this scene at least four days, except that this scene was never written. No word of it was written – and we discussed everybody's life, each one's character, their background, their position at this moment in the story, what they would think about everything – and then sat down and cranked the camera, and every actor made up his lines as he went along. The scene lasts three and a half minutes or something in its entirety and was written by the actors as we went along. I'm very proud of them for it. It has an extraordinary effect, entirely due to their preparation for doing it.'

A study of the novel and the screenplay contradicts Welles's remarks: with a few differences, the scene comprises the first part of Chapter Sixteen in the novel. Jack (a Falstaffian character whose name in the book is George Amberson) does not appear in this scene in the book; his lines are taken from a speech of his in Chapter Fifteen and from one of George Minafer's in Chapter Sixteen. And the scene *was* written out in the script – it covers pages 64 to 68. The only improvisations were the occasional lines about George's eating: 'Quit bolting your food . . . Don't eat so fast, George . . . Want some more milk? – No, thanks . . . You're going to get fat. – Can't help that!' But Welles is correct in his praise of the actors: the scene *seems* off-the-cuff because of their skilful interweaving of set dialogue and impromptu remarks. Agnes Moorehead

The Magnificent Ambersons: (*above*) dinner at the Ambersons' (Ray Collins, Joseph Cotten, Richard Bennett, Tim Holt); (*below*) 'Quit bolting your food.' (Agnes Moorehead, Ray Collins, Tim Holt)

again sets and changes her tone with great concentration, and the slight stiffness of some of Tim Holt's and Ray Collins's deliveries actually adds to the verisimilitude.

The scene ends with a fade-out on Jack's 'I really don't know of anything much Fanny *has* got – except her feeling for Eugene,' and a cut to a blacksmith hammering steel in Eugene's factory. But there have been cuts made between these scenes. In the script George, looking out of the window (as he now is on the fade-out), shouts 'Holy cats!' and dashes out to look at a row of excavations on the mansion lawn. He stands in the rain, furious; Jack arrives a moment later to shield him with an umbrella and to defend the Major's decision to break up the lot for housing. This was to fade to George's buggy and Eugene's car parked outside the entrance of the 'MORGAN HORSELESS CARRIAGES' factory. From *there* Welles intended to make the cut to the tracking shot of the group inside the factory.

The loss of the excavation scenes – and of later scenes which touch on the Major's thrift measures – robs the film of some of its most acute points of family-town conflict. The factory scene, with its intense workmen pulling ropes and pushing automobiles, its car on display, and its process screen showing large machines in the background – all this clamour sets off most effectively the small focus of the scene: Fanny's anguished face turning slowly towards the camera as Isabel and Eugene reminisce about 'the original Morgan Invincible', which stands behind them. A brief excised scene was to have shown George and Lucy getting into their carriage and joking about their 'sentimental' elders.

After the next scene in the released film, the brief conversation between Isabel and Eugene on the mansion lawn, which Welles had intended to come three scenes later, George is shown driving Lucy through the town. Welles jump-cuts from their carriage following in the exhaust of Eugene's car to the carriage trotting steadily along the street; the music conveys the same jaunty feeling as the cut. This long tracking shot is a famous example of Welles's camera *vs* character counterpoint. At the end of the shot the camera gains slowly on the carriage, and we can see that the dolly has been rolling on streetcar tracks. Welles goes so far to acknowledge the camera's involvement in the scene as actually to show the wheel of the dolly (another carriage) in the lower left-hand corner of the screen.

The Magnificent Ambersons: the Morgan horseless carriage

The camera halts; George gallops the carriage out of the frame right; the Major's buggy follows and a quick dissolve shows Jack and the Major in conversation inside the buggy. This procession of the generations – first the automobile, then George, then the Major – is a superb visual metaphor. The buggy scene has been truncated, and the dialogue indicates that the reason was a reference to the excavations. After the Major's line about the town rolling over his heart and 'burying it under', the following exchange is missing:

Major: When I think of those devilish workmen digging up my lawn, yelling around my house —

Jack: Never mind, Father. Don't think of it. When things are a nuisance, it's a good idea not to keep remembering 'em.

Major: (*murmurs*) I *try* not to. I try to keep remembering that I won't be remembering anything very long. (*Becomes mirthful and slaps his knee*) Not so very long now, my boy. Not so very long now. Not so very long!

The next scene retained in the film is the dinner-table argument, but the buggy scene was to have dissolved into a conversation on the mansion veranda. Bicycles and surreys flash by in the evening, disrupted by an occasional noisy automobile. George is brooding, oblivious to the conversation. The five new houses on the lawn have progressed, one already completed. Fanny tells Isabel that autos are a fad, 'like roller skates'. 'Besides,' she goes on, 'people just won't stand for them after a while. I shouldn't be surprised to see a law passed forbidding the sale of automobiles the way there is with concealed weapons.' When Isabel counters with a gentle question about her sincerity in telling Eugene that she had enjoyed the afternoon's drive, Fanny says that she 'didn't say it so very enthusiastically', and that it 'hardly seems time yet – to me' for anyone to get the idea that Eugene had pleased her.

A very uneasy silence follows, the only sound the creaking of Fanny's wicker rocking-chair. 'A series of human shrieks could have been little more eloquent of emotional disturbance,' Tarkington notes at this point. Then Isabel notices that across the street Mrs Johnson is spying on them from her bedroom window with a pair of opera glasses. With a laughing remark, Isabel goes inside. Fanny expresses thinly concealed reproach over Isabel's 'queer' behaviour, her violation of mourning 'on the *very* anniversary of Wilbur's death!' George ignores her as she clangs the door shut, leaving him alone. Then follows the scene which, for all the beauty it must have had, evidently prompted RKO to cut this sequence – it probably sent the preview audience into hysterics.

As George sits brooding, Lucy 'appears in old-fashioned transparency (the shadowy ghost figure from the silents). She throws herself on the steps at his feet.' The visionary Lucy begs George to forgive her and assures him that she will never again listen to her father's opinions. George solemnly pardons her but, realizing that he has been talking to himself, swings his feet down to the floor of the veranda: 'Pardon nothing!' Then he pictures Lucy 'as she probably really is at this moment; sitting on her own front porch in the moonlight with four or five boys, all of them laughing most likely, and some idiot probably playing a guitar.' He paces the stone floor furiously, muttering 'Riff-raff!' over and over. This was to have dissolved to the lawn scene.

The climax of the drama, George's announcement that automobiles are 'a useless nuisance', comes in the dinner sequence, the next retained in the film and reportedly Welles's favourite in the film. This is George's first formal step. From this point on he is determined to wreck his mother's romance. Chiefly remarkable about the argument is the brilliance of the montage: the first few shots keep George in the background, on the periphery of the conversation. He blurts out his line off-screen while Eugene and the Major are shown talking; Welles cuts to Jack withdrawing his hand from the table, then to Isabel holding her breath, her head slightly back and her eyes partly closed. Only then does he show George, who repeats what he has said and adds that 'they had no business to be invented'. After a reprimand from Jack (which in the novel is given by the Major, Jack being absent), George is shown in sullen isolation. In the background is a giant cross-bar shadow, similar to those which appear throughout *Kane* at the most ominous moments: the opening, the breakfast montage, Susan's suicide attempt, the ending. Welles also made extensive use of this in *Othello*, showing Iago's cage time and again during the course of the action.

Eugene's speech about automobiles changing men's minds is chiefly significant for its effect on his and George's faces, which are shown in an exchange of several close-ups. Eugene is agreeing with George that automobiles 'had no business to be invented', but their faces say otherwise. Eugene excuses himself and leaves, Fanny darting after him, and on Jack's return through the door a moment later the camera pans from George on the left and Isabel on the right to a shot framing Jack (in the background) and George (now on the right). After another reprimand from Jack, George throws down his napkin and bolts for the door – the camera swinging right with his motion, Isabel rising at the same moment. Then a quick cut to George slamming open the door to the hall, where Fanny intercepts him. This rapid, precise cutting helps the acting and the carefully sculptured lighting to establish George's increasingly angry mood.

The staircase scene which follows is one of the most effective crane shots in Welles's work. George follows Fanny ('It's always Fanny, ridiculous old Fanny – always – always!') through huge shadows; they halt on the first landing, the camera tilted slightly to the right as George shakes her. This is one of Agnes Moorehead's greatest scenes. She simultaneously conveys profound anger at George, envy of Isabel, transparent self-pity, and sympathy for George. She says that the romance 'wouldn't have amounted to anything if Wilbur had lived', and he asks incredulously, 'You mean

The Magnificent Ambersons: the staircase scene (Agnes Moorehead, Tim Holt)

Morgan might have married *you*?' She gulps – her head back, her fingers doing a nervous pirouette on the railing – and, with exquisite inflection, says, 'No ... because I don't know that ... I'd have accepted him.'

George dashes off, leaving Fanny terrified. As he grills the old gossip, Mrs Johnson, the camera eavesdrops, reframing the characters five times in its almost complete revolution around the room. The transition from this scene is a visual shock like that of the screeching cockatoo in *Citizen Kane*: George in his dark suit strides out of the frame left – the white-dressed Mrs Johnson stands outraged for a moment – then a cut to Jack's bath-water streaming out of the tap as he and it make similar groaning sounds. After George's portentous exit from the bathroom (Jack's comment, 'For heaven's sake, don't be so theatrical!' is also the artist's humorous comment on his work, as was Kane's line, 'I had no idea you had this flair for melodrama, Emily'), three scenes have been cut:

Isabel's door opens as George walks into the hall. He steps into a

The Magnificent Ambersons: Tim Holt in one of the cut scenes

shadow as he hears her voice. She opens the door to his room, sees that he is gone, and returns to her room. He noiselessly goes to the stairs and up to the ballroom. The next scene is similar to famous shots in *Kane* and *The Lady from Shanghai*: 'Moonlight, coming through the glass ceiling, floods the room. George walks to the centre of the ballroom and stands there, reflected in the pier-glass mirrors that line all sides of the room.' Like Kane he sees the endless reflection of his own ego, and this, his most acute moment of consciousness, is interrupted by Isabel's footfall and voice.

She stops on the stairs, and he has nowhere to go. Her timid attempts at wishing him goodnight are answered in perfunctory monosyllables. She walks away, and the scene fades to George unwrapping a framed photograph of his father the next day in the drawing-room. He whispers brokenly, 'Poor, poor father! Poor man, I'm glad you didn't know!' He walks to the window and sits looking through the curtains. Through the gloomy silence Isabel's voice can be heard in a song:

Lord Bateman was a noble lord,
A noble lord of high degree;
And he sailed West and he sailed East,
Far countries for to see ...

The words to this foreshadowing of Eugene's visit become indistinct, change to a whistle, to a hum, and then drift out of hearing. George stares out of the window.

The next part of the sequence is retained in the released film: Eugene arriving, George watching from the window, George opening the door and ordering him to leave. 'Perhaps you'll understand *this*,' he says, and slams the door. For about ten seconds Morgan stands still, seen through the frosted glass. Then he leaves, and George goes back into the house, slamming the door of the entrance hall behind him. Missing here is a scene in the drawing-room in which Isabel, still whistling 'Lord Bateman', finds George sitting in the gloom. Hearing the doorbell ring and being told by the maid that it was a pedlar, she asks George what the earlier 'pedlar' (George's explanation to the maid) had been selling. 'He didn't say,' George answers. A tense moment follows when Isabel notices the silver-framed picture George has placed on the table. She asks if it is Lucy, but on approaching gives a long, just audible 'Oh!'. George is silent, and she says, 'That was nice of you, Georgie. I ought to have had it framed myself, when I gave it to you.' She puts her hand on his shoulder, withdraws it, and leaves. After a while George follows.

Dissolves were to connect two short scenes of him in the hall peering at his mother, who is waiting at the window of the drawing-room for Eugene to arrive. A third scene was to show him leaving his room as Jack rings the doorbell off-camera. In the film as it stands, George walking away from Eugene dissolves into Isabel waiting (which was to have been the next shot in this intended sequence). The framed picture of Wilbur is prominently placed in this scene. Isabel rises and goes into the hall. Welles then cuts to Jack leading her through the hall to tell her what George has done. A ponderous upward tilt of the camera, underscored by a heavy musical chord and huge shadows, shows Fanny dashing down the stairs to keep George from disturbing his mother. After this a short scene of Isabel comforting her son in his room, a dark, pathetic moment in which she whispers, 'You mustn't be troubled, darling,' has been cut.

The letter scenes which follow do not come off well, except for the device of dissolving a tilted shot of the empty hall (through which Jack and Isabel had walked moments earlier) between Eugene writing the letter and Isabel reading it. Neither scene was shot by Welles, and the subsequent confrontation between mother and son was reshot, apparently to mute George's reaction to Eugene and Isabel's marriage plans. In the script, George calls the letter 'offensive' and tells her he is 'doing what my father would ask me to do' and is 'protecting' her. She capitulates – but not easily, not mawkishly, as she does in the scene now in the film. Isabel was to have left the room in tears, leaving George to examine himself in a mirror and whisper Hamlet's speech beginning "Tis not alone my inky cloak, good mother ...' Then two brief scenes were to show her writing a letter surrendering to George and him reading it.

The long tracking shot along the street with George and Lucy, the film's next scene, is concerned not with a combat between two wills, as was their earlier trip through the town, but with Lucy's cool domination over George. Hence the camera maintains a *constant* distance from them. Welles's Stroheim-like naturalism dominates here – in the windows of the buildings behind them can be seen reflections of the buildings across the street, as in the earlier shot. But things are different: more people are on the sidewalks, the pedestrians' pace is faster, the traffic heavier. Several Model-As are among the reflected vehicles. The earlier shot had included more residences than stores: in place of the earlier scene's homely hardware store are a drapery shop, a large bank, a movie theatre, a drugstore. A warehouse has acquired a second story since we saw it last. On the boards outside the theatre are posters for a Méliès movie – a tribute from one cinematic magician to another – and for 'Jack Holt in *Explosion*', a reference to Tim Holt's father, a former stuntman who started his long Western career in 1919, fourteen years after this scene takes place.

This shot is the oddest in the film. Some critics have thought that Lucy's rather puzzling indifference to George would have been better explained had the film not been cut, and this is true. Welles intended the scene to be in its present place, but it should be recalled that the last time Lucy had appeared was in the cut scene of

George's 'vision'. At the close of that scene she was seen being wooed by four or five other boys, and if that had remained, her attitude here would be more easily understood. As the shot begins, George asks her, 'Haven't you —' and she cuts in, 'Haven't I what?' He drops the matter and it is apparent that Eugene hasn't told her about what happened the day before (she wouldn't be speaking to George if he had).

But all that now exists in the film to explain her attitude are her comments about the quarrel they had had, and how they hadn't spoken to each other 'all the way home from a long, long drive'. It is hard for the audience to connect this with the carriage ride through town, which happened more than a dozen scenes earlier. Lucy teases George about the absurdity of their earlier behaviour, and the confused audience is left to speculate over whether she has or hasn't heard about Eugene's expulsion after all. And when George walks away and Welles cuts to a close-up of Lucy which includes only the dark parts of her outfit – her collar, hat, and muff – this tonal change, which would have been such a brilliant formal effect had the film retained its original structure, only provides more confusion. And when she faints in the drugstore... Since this sequence is intended both to counterpoint a much earlier scene and to refer to a scene which has been removed, it is unsuccessful.

The next three scenes were cut and the fourth evidently reshot. The first was a night shot of the five new houses on the mansion lawn. In front of them passes a steady stream of automobiles, with now and then a bicycle or, at long intervals, a surrey or buggy. The Major and Fanny are seen on the veranda in long shot, then more closely. Their dialogue is concerned with the Major's financial problems, which he had tried to remedy (without much luck) by having the houses built, and with Fanny's and Jack's investment in the headlight company. The dialogue shifts to an ironic exchange:

Major (gravely):   Isabel wants to come home. Her letters are full of it. Jack writes me she talks of nothing else.
   No answer from Fanny.
Major: She's wanted to come for a long while. She ought to come while she can stand the journey.
   Another pause.
Fanny: People are making such enormous fortunes out of everything to

do with motor cars, it does seem as if – I wrote Jack I'd think it over seriously.

Major (*laughing*): Well, Fanny, maybe we'll be partners. How about it? And millionaires, too!

The scene fades to a chauffeur-driven car starting up the driveway of the great Georgian Morgan mansion. Another shot shows Lucy and Jack inside the car. Lucy doesn't quite understand when Jack tells her, 'Here's the Amberson mansion again, only it's Georgian instead of nondescript Romanesque; but it's just the same Amberson mansion my father built long before you were born.' She laughs 'as a friend should', and they go into the house. An interior scene shows him teasing her about still being a belle of the ball, and about her recent refusal to become engaged to one of George's boyhood friends. She laughs, a little embarrassed.

Jack: Well, you're pretty refreshingly out of the smoke up here.

Lucy (*laughing*): For a little while. Until it comes and we have to move out farther.

Jack: No, you'll stay here. It'll be somebody else who'll move out farther.

Then the scene dissolves to Jack telling Eugene and Lucy that Isabel wants to come home from abroad, and that she ought to be in a wheelchair. As the film now stands, Lucy's fainting fades out and into a slow zoom shot (the only zoom in the film) of Jack and Lucy walking up the steps of the Morgan mansion. The dialogue is the archest kind of plot exposition: 'Mighty nice of you, Lucy, you and Eugene, to have me over to your new house my first day back. – You'll probably find the old town rather dull after Paris.' The studio had carefully removed all the scenes dealing with the new houses on the lawn, and as a consequence found themselves with a five-year gap to explain (it is now 1910, and the fainting scene occurred in 1905, just before George and Isabel left for Europe). So they decided to shoot a new scene, which leads most clumsily into the completely static discussion in the Morgan library, a scene which probably fitted well into the original film, but here is conspicuously slow.

After the short scenes of Isabel arriving at the station and being driven home ('Changed – so changed'), the script indicates a scene outside her second-floor bedroom. The Major querulously demands to see his daughter, and when he is admitted into the room, Fanny asks George if Eugene can see Isabel. George abruptly refuses, and Fanny tells Eugene. He asks if he could only 'look into the room and see her for just a second', but finally capitulates. These scenes were rewritten into the present one, which shows George refusing Morgan at the foot of the stairs, Morgan defying him, and then Fanny saying, 'I don't think you should right now – the doctor said . . .' and breaking into tears. Jack agrees with her, and Eugene leaves, Fanny following him with her eyes.

This change of emphasis is unfortunate. Shifting the final decision, however inconclusively, to Fanny and Jack lessens one of the book's (and script's) most powerful themes, George's guilt over denying his mother's last request. The next shot is of George's face superimposed on the window as Eugene walks to his car: this seems to imply that George had *ordered* Fanny and Jack's decision, which would contradict the scene on the stairs. And if Fanny is denying Eugene's request only because of her own envy, why does Jack also deny Eugene? The scene has been obscured both in the writing and (apparently) in reshooting.

The nurse's voice tells George that his mother wants to see him, and Welles immediately cuts from the superimposed shot of George's face to his actual face turning away from the window. This is a powerful effect, a visual shock that in its complete reversal of George's image shows how deeply he is shaken. (Compare this to the bullets shattering the mirror images of Bannister and his wife at the end of *The Lady from Shanghai*.) Achieving this effect allows Welles to understate the deathbed scene. George shows more shame than grief, the grief having been shown at the window, as he listens to his mother's pathetic questions. 'Dear, did you – get something to eat?' 'Yes, mother.' 'All you needed?' 'Yes, mother.' When she says that she would have liked to have seen Eugene just once, George turns away in deep shame. Isabel's eyes strain to see him leave.

Her face dissolves into perhaps the most powerful shot in Welles's entire *œuvre*. The slow dissolve, accompanied by the two contrasting musical motifs used in *Citizen Kane* – the deep brass of the 'power' motif and the vibraphone 'Rosebud' motif – reveals the Major sleeping fitfully on George's bed. He suddenly awakes, the music hinting that he has been dreaming, and rises in terror. The camera makes an hallucinatory pull slightly away from him, Jack crosses in front of him, the camera holds on the Major for a moment

The Magnificent Ambersons: George with his mother (Tim Holt, Dolores Costello)

and then pans right as he totters off towards Jack, who by now has almost left the frame – suddenly Fanny throws her arms around George, who is standing in the extreme foreground with his back to the camera. 'George! She loved you! She loved you!'. George's face is not shown, just his back, and Welles again achieves the objective-subjective fusion of the reporter's scenes in *Kane*. The two tiny camera movements achieve such a strong effect because of their careful timing with the characters' movements, with the shock of Fanny's entrance, and because of the surreal, dreamlike compression of the scene: once the Major wakes, it is over in seconds. Like Kane's hand entering the frame to slap Susan, it is an epiphany.

A dissolve was then to have flickered (as a fade does now) to the Major seated in front of an unseen fireplace, the light of the flames playing on his face. He stares straight into the camera, which is at a slight low angle, like Mr Clay ruminating on power and destiny many years later in *The Immortal Story*.

'And now,' Welles narrates, 'Major Amberson was engaged in the profoundest thinking of his life . . .' Richard Bennett, whom Welles had brought out of retirement to play the Major and who died two years after the film was made, had trouble retaining his lines, and his eyesight was so bad that he couldn't read from a blackboard during the scene. *Collier's* reported that Welles had recited the Major's speech ('It must be in – the sun – ') on a record which Bennett then took home to memorize.

'I play it over,' he explained to Joseph Cotten, 'and I take portions of it and write them down and study them. I do it over and over, word by word.'

'Are you getting them?' Cotten asked.

'Not a bloody blasted one of them!' cried Bennett proudly.

When the scene was shot, Welles stood just outside the frame and prompted Bennett every few words. When the sound was processed, Welles's voice was eliminated. This partially explains the pauses between the phrases, which have such a moving effect when combined with the sombre music, the slow track forward and the sculptural lighting on the Major's deeply-lined face. The fade-out also flickers, an effect repeated several times during the film: the lighting on the character's face (here from the fire) is the strongest in the shot, so the dissolve or fade makes the face appear disembodied.

This fades to the haunting scene of Jack's farewell to George in the railroad station. After that, the structure of the film has been changed completely.

The following is the film's original ending sequence:

1. Major at fireside.
2. Jack bidding George farewell at railroad station.
3. George walks through town; dissolves of buildings; people in a car jeer at him; the camera follows him to the mansion and then wanders through it; he kneels at his mother's bed and asks forgiveness; exterior views of mansion.
4. George with Fanny in mansion kitchen and ballroom.
5. George refuses a job offer from lawyer Bronson and asks help in getting a job in a dynamite factory.
6. Eugene and Lucy walking in their garden.
7. George injured in auto accident.
8. Accident seen as newspaper story.
9. Eugene reads story; leaves for hospital.

10. Later, Eugene visits Fanny in a boarding house. They discuss Lucy and George (soon to be married) while a phonograph plays a serio-comic song about the city. Eugene gets into his car, takes a last look back at Fanny against the skyline of the changed city. The End.
11. Credits.

The following is the ending as it now stands:

1. Major at fireside.
2. Jack and George at station.
3. Eugene and Lucy walking in their garden.
4. George with Fanny in mansion kitchen and ballroom.
5. George in Bronson's office.
6. George walks through town; dissolves of buildings; he kneels at the bed and asks forgiveness.
7. George injured in auto accident.
8. Accident seen as newspaper story.
9. Eugene in his study with Lucy; they leave for hospital.
10. Eugene and Fanny in hospital corridor.
11. Credits.

The first thing to be said about the original ending sequence is that it was fluid. A static scene (Jack's farewell to George) is followed by a montage (George walking home), which is followed by a violent scene (Fanny's hysteria), and so forth. The scenes as they stand now are jerky and have only a haphazard chronological continuity. The scene which suffers the most from this displacement is the quite lovely shot of Eugene and Lucy walking through their garden. In its present place as the third in a succession of nearly static scenes it seems oppressively slow and, consequently, laboured and coy. But as Welles intended it, as a let-down from the dynamic scenes of George's repentance and Fanny's hysteria, it would have been most effective.

Furthermore, George's job at the dynamite factory seems to last an incongruously short time before he is injured in the auto accident, which in turn is weakened in effect. As Welles planned it, the garden scene was to have intervened between Bronson's office and the accident. The Morgans' talk would have conditioned the viewer's awareness that George has been on the job for some time, as indeed he has: the script indicates that a year has elapsed. The accident, in the novel's words, was 'so commonplace and inconsequent that it was a comedy', but following immediately after his 'comeuppance', that moving shot of him kneeling in the deserted house, the accident seems so *consequent* upon his 'comeuppance' that it is absurd. But the audience doesn't have time to reflect on the silliness of its placement, for immediately after the newspaper inserts reporting the accident come the campy ending shots directed, according to Bogdanovich, by Freddie Fleck, Welles's assistant director. Strangely enough, of all the reviewers only Manny Farber in *The Nation* seemed to have been bothered by these last three shots, attributing the 'hearts-and-flowers finish' to 'blundering editing'.

The thematic reversal in these last two scenes, not to mention the stylistic let-down, is appalling. After a scene in Morgan's study in which Anne Baxter prods a hypnotized-looking Joseph Cotten into striding out of the frame with her, we are asked to agree, as Eugene informs Fanny outside George's hospital room, that 'everything's going to be all right'. And, thanks to the meretricious direction, Fanny seems to have become Eugene's 'true love'.

The book's rather protracted denouement has Eugene going to a medium and believing for a while that he has contacted Isabel, who tells him to 'be kind'. Then he returns home to see George, who asks his forgiveness. It ends with the sentimental note that through Eugene, Isabel 'had brought her boy under shelter again. Her eyes would look wistful no more.' Fleck's scene ends with Eugene telling Fanny that through him Isabel had 'brought her boy under shelter again and that I'd been true at last to my true love.' On these last words, the camera swings to Fanny's face, then back to include Eugene. The implication, reinforced by a sudden burst of music and a little sigh from Fanny, is that Eugene has loved her all along.

The power of individual scenes persists through the chaotic structure of the present ending sequence. Foremost is Agnes Moorehead's great scene in the kitchen and hall of the deserted mansion. Welles rehearsed her over and over until she actually was in hysterics when it was filmed. As George drags her through the hall, shaking her back to her senses, the camera tracks rapidly back with them through three rooms and into the dining-room, gaining increasingly on them and finally pulling away to distance us from a scene of an intensity seldom equalled on film.

The dissolves of George walking through 'the strange streets of a strange city' are done with the camera playing George (originally he

The Magnificent Ambersons: the kitchen scene (Agnes Moorehead, Tim Holt)

was to have appeared, seen from the back, in the first shot of the series; the camera moves faster than he does, tracking in so close that his body forms a dark screen for a dissolve): this objective effect reinforces the strangeness of the dirty buildings, telephone wires and rundown houses ('New Hope Apartments'). The montage was to have been at least three times as long as that in the present film: shots of a cleaning and dye house, a funeral home and a lodge (once scenes of George's boyhood, the narrator says) have been cut, as has a short scene in which a carload of youngsters jeer at him as he walks down what had once been 'Amberson Boulevard' and is now '10th Street'. From the angle of the people in the car, George is seen muttering 'Riff-raff!' The camera pulls slowly away, then faster, 'as though it is the car', leaving George a tiny figure in the distance – another insult from the automobile.

This dissolves to shots of him entering the mansion, which in turn dissolve to a shot in which the camera wanders slowly through the dismantled house. It recapitulates the reception-room, the kitchen, returns up the staircase, stops for a moment, pans down to the heavy library doors (behind which Isabel had learned of Eugene's expulsion), and after a short pause pans back and continues, even more slowly, up the stairs to the second-floor hall and to the closed door of Isabel's room. The door swings open and we see that nothing has been changed. Then this extraordinary shot was to fade out. During this part of the montage the narrator has been saying:

The city had rolled over his heart and buried it under as it rolled over the Major's and the Ambersons' and buried them under to the last vestige.

Tonight would be the last night that he and Fanny were to spend in the house which the Major had forgotten to deed to Isabel. Tomorrow they were to 'move out'.

Tomorrow everything would be gone: the very space in which tonight was still Isabel's room would be cut into new shapes by new walls and floors and ceilings. And if space itself can be haunted as memory is haunted, then it may be that some impressionable, overworked woman in a 'kitchenette', after turning out the light, will seem to see a young man kneeling in the darkness, with arms outstretched through the wall, clutching at the covers of a shadowy bed. It may seem to her that she hears the faint cry, over and over —

Now the screen was to fade into the dark shot of the back of George's head, which, as the camera retreats, reveals him kneeling in his mother's room. After the narration which remains in the film ('. . . George Amberson Minafer had got his comeuppance. He'd got it three times filled and running over . . .'), the scene was to dissolve slowly to shots of the old mansion, windows broken, front door ajar, and 'idiot salacity' smeared upon the pillars and stonework of the veranda.

The mutilation of the film is, of course, unconscionable, but the first half is relatively intact, and in that and in the isolated power of the other scenes *The Ambersons* will continue to live. As Truffaut has said, 'If Flaubert re-read *Don Quixote* each year, why can't we re-see *The Ambersons* whenever possible?'

The film as we see it is quite hectic, more melodramatic than it had been; the studio naturally retained the 'plot' scenes at the expense of the quieter, more ironic shots which Welles himself has called 'the whole heart of the picture really' (the veranda scenes, the missing two-thirds of the town montage, the camera moving through the empty house, etc.). With the loss of the excavation scenes and other shots of the spreading town, the film concentrates more on the family itself than was intended, and the ironic bite arising from the Ambersons' gradual de-eminence in the town has been lessened. The exact pace of the planned film has become ragged and somewhat exhausting, but enough of Welles's overall conception remains for it to be apparent from the film itself just how great a work it was before RKO got cold feet. Today Robert Wise feels that no serious harm was done: 'We had a picture with major problems, and I feel all of us tried sincerely to keep the best of Welles's concept and still lick the problem. Since *Ambersons* has become something of a classic, I think it's now apparent we didn't "mutilate" Orson's film.'

Wise felt that the war had prevented the audience's interest in the film's subject matter. Which war? The New York *Times* spoke for its public when it wrote, 'In a world brimful of momentous drama beggaring serious screen treatment, it does seem that Mr Welles is imposing when he asks moviegoers to become emotionally disturbed over the decline of such minor-league American aristocracy as the Ambersons represented in the late Eighteen Seventies.'

The missing footage reportedly exists in the Paramount Studios film library (which acquired RKO's films in 1958), but a scholar would have to dig through literally millions of feet of film to find it, since the collection is not properly catalogued. Kane's loss of Rosebud was no sadder than this. Welles has talked of shooting two new reels to make the ending coherent, using the surviving actors as they are today, but admits that he is getting depressed by the number of his unfinished projects.

6: Finding a New Style

Journey Into Fear

Besides letting Welles direct films in which he would not appear, such as *The Magnificent Ambersons*, George Schaefer asked him to supervise the production of films which he would not direct but in which he and his stock company of Mercury actors would appear. The first of such projects, *The Way to Santiago*, was written by Welles and John Houseman from Arthur Calder-Marshall's novel and was to follow *Citizen Kane* in 1941. Norman Foster was to direct, and Gregg Toland to photograph it. An anti-fascist adventure story set in Mexico, starring Welles as an allied agent and Dolores Del Rio, then his fiancée, as a lady spy – something of a precursor to Hitchcock's *Notorious*, but with the male partner drugged by Nazis and rescued by the woman – the film was cancelled because of political complications.

During the shooting of *The Ambersons*, Welles's company began work on *Journey Into Fear*, a war thriller set in the Near East, directed by Foster from a script by Welles and Joseph Cotten based on a novel by Eric Ambler. Like *The Way to Santiago*, the story has much of Welles in it – he plays the first of his costume villains, a Turkish police chief named Colonel Haki who bears an uncanny resemblance to Joseph Stalin – but it is also in the nature of a *divertissement*, a semi-serious relaxation from the demands of his more personal projects. Also, presumably, these more conventional films would help pay for the films Welles would direct.

A degree of confusion has persisted over Welles's directorial contribution to *Journey Into Fear*. Everett Sloane said that 'we did all

Journey Into Fear: Joseph Cotten and shipmates

Orson's scenes first and he directed them, then Norman did the rest of it. I think it retains much of Orson's original conception of the picture.' Welles amplifies this: 'For the first five sequences I was on the set and decided angles; from then on, I often said where to put the camera, described the framings, made light tests ... I designed the film but can't properly be called the director.' The story resembles those of several later Welles films. Cotten plays a naïve American engineer dragged off by the Nazis to prevent him from arming Turkish ships; like O'Hara in *The Lady from Shanghai*, Welles's archetypal 'innocent', and Joseph K. in *The Trial*, he stumbles foolishly into more and more danger while trying to understand why he is being pursued. Welles is in a position of power similar to that of the Advocate in *The Trial*, and Cotten resembles K. in his impeccably business-like appearance and in his self-conscious jesting about a grim situation. The incomprehension of Cotten's wife (Ruth Warrick) is agreeably humorous, and the film is all but stolen by a greasy, silent, baby-faced villain played by Jack Moss, who looks almost exactly like one of the executioners in *The Trial*. If the film doesn't hold together as entertainment or have any special thematic compulsion, it serves at least as a very rough draft for some of Welles's later films.

One of its virtues is that, unlike Welles's disastrous *The Stranger*, it doesn't take its absurd situation too seriously. When the villain sits across the table from Cotten and starts to gobble his dinner menacingly, Cotten furtively tosses some salt over his shoulder. Welles's Haki is a joke pure and simple, and Agnes Moorehead and Sloane turn in amusing performances. Some of the fey humour of the script is more tedious than charming, however, and Cotten's characterization becomes distractingly blasé. As in Hitchcock's *Torn Curtain*, which has a quite similar story, the insipidness of the couple tends to negate our involvement in the action, and whatever urgency their relationship may be presumed to possess is submerged by the power of set-pieces – murder during the blackout of a magic act (a good idea indifferently directed) and a gun duel on a window ledge during a blinding rainstorm. What finally makes *Journey Into Fear* inconsequential is its lack of *wholeness*. Good acting is dissipated by clumsy pacing of dialogue; the lighting shifts jarringly from high-key to chiaroscuro; the structure is too episodic. In retrospect, we can see that Welles did to this film what other people did to *The Ambersons*: tried to make little 'improvements' here and there and in the process destroyed whatever stylistic unity it might have attained. The danger of outside interference would have to strike Welles in the cruellest way, and too late to save *Journey Into Fear*.

It's All True

It's All True, the semi-documentary South American film Welles shot in 1942, remains one of the great mysteries of film scholarship. Welles was fired by RKO before the shooting was completed; much of the footage was eventually destroyed (several reels were literally sunk in the Pacific Ocean), and what remains is entombed in the Paramount vaults. A long series of attempts by Welles to reclaim the footage has failed; as recently as 1969, he was trying to get it packaged as a television show.

Recent articles describing the film have served only to deepen the confusion over what it contained. Obviously, the only person who can give a full account of the film is Welles himself, and since I have

Journey Into Fear: gun duel in a rainstorm (Joseph Cotten, Jack Moss)

not seen *It's All True*, I refer the reader to Peter Bogdanovich's book-length interview with the director. Briefly, the film, shot partially in colour, was in three sections: *The Story of Bonito, the Bull*, about a Mexican boy and his pet bull, who enters the bull-ring (co-directed by Norman Foster); *Jangadeiros*, recreating an epic 1,650-mile journey by raft of four Brazilian fishermen (one of them was killed during the shooting) to protest poor living conditions; and *The Samba Story*, tracing the folk dance from its origins in voodoo to its full flowering at the Rio Carnival.

Jane Eyre

An unexpectedly rich film, *Jane Eyre* is important not only because it made Welles a star (enabling him to support himself as an actor and survive directorial incapacity) but because Welles seems to have influenced much of the direction, and to a more salutary effect than in *Journey Into Fear*. Robert Stevenson, now a Disney director turning out an occasional pleasant picture such as *Mary Poppins*, was in charge, but as a columnist of the time reported, Welles was 'directing the director of *Jane Eyre* on how to direct'. The script, out of Charlotte Brontë by Aldous Huxley, Houseman and Stevenson, was excellent, the supporting cast (Joan Fontaine, Henry Daniell, Agnes Moorehead) and the role of Edward Rochester well

89

suited for the demands of a full-blown theatrical treatment. We do not have the feeling, as we do in *Journey Into Fear*, of Welles condescending to the material, and if it is not quite all of a piece, *Jane Eyre* is more than intermittently powerful and moving. If Welles had been the director, a fully integrated film might have resulted, though the material tends to bring out some of the more purely self-indulgent aspects of his personality and would have required painstaking refinement and stylization to be a complete success.

Some of the reviewers objected to Welles's approach to Rochester. Walter Kerr claimed that Eddie Anderson would have been more appropriate. James Agee referred to Welles's 'road-operatic sculpturings of body, cloak and diction, his eyes glinting in the Rembrandt gloom, at every chance, like side-orders of jelly. It is possible to enjoy his performance as dead-pan period parody; I imagine he did. I might have more if I hadn't wanted, instead, to see a good performance.' The film would no doubt have been more controlled had Laurence Olivier played Rochester and Welles directed, but I think that Agee's complaint would better apply to a less expressionistic, more literary production such as William Wyler's *Wuthering Heights*, which is brought alive by Gregg Toland's photography and Olivier's acting but becomes ludicrous when Heathcliff carries the dying Cathy to look at the moors, a scene Welles probably could have pulled off with *élan*. Elsewhere Agee notes the lack of 'symbolic resonance'. This is the objection that reviewers, most of whom cringe in the presence of unabashedly theatrical presentation, demanding something either parodistic or more 'subtle', make to Welles's most operatic roles – Macbeth, Othello, Arkadin, the Advocate, Falstaff. They attack the acting as if it were separable from *mise-en-scène*. One might as well attack Shakespeare's characters for speaking blank verse.

The critics' objections, however mistaken in principle, retain a certain validity here, though, because of the hybrid nature of the direction. The attempt at operatic stylization is simply not consistent. That lovely actress Joan Fontaine, for example, is a perfect childlike foil to Welles in a scene such as their meeting on the moors, Welles rearing up on his horse and tumbling into the murk; or the scene in which Welles questions her about her past life, and she wins his grudging respect by refusing to be bullied. But the

Jane Eyre: Welles as Rochester, Joan Fontaine as Jane

rhythm of the film is off; close-ups of Jane come at the slightest provocation (Welles generally avoids close-ups), and the intimacy of these moments often becomes grotesque when Welles is given a matching close-up and slips into 'road-operatic' mannerism which rings false in a context of naturalistic interplay. The best scenes are those of the most exquisite exaggeration and the darkest humour, such as the early scene in which the little Jane is introduced to her schoolmaster (Daniell at his most unctuously Calvinistic), with Agnes Moorehead icily fondling a monstrously fat little boy eating chocolates – a scene which recalls the glossily Gothic opening of Sternberg's *The Scarlet Empress* (a film Welles evidently much admires, since he also re-creates scenes from it in *Kane* and *The Immortal Story*), and a fascinating glimpse of what Welles might have been able to do with the entire film.

Jane awakening to an eerily militaristic morning toilet in the girls' school; the master berating her as a heathen as she stands on a stool before the assembled girls; Jane and an astonishingly beautiful little girl (Elizabeth Taylor in her prime) doing penance in a driving rainstorm; Jane tenderly going to sleep with the sick little girl and waking to find that the girl's hand has gone cold; Rochester saying, 'Parson, close your book – there'll be no wedding today' and exposing his mad wife to Jane; the closing scenes of his blindness and miraculous revivification: all these are suggestive of Welles's touch.

There remains also Bernard Herrmann's magnificent score, which almost succeeds in unifying the erratic visual texture and justifying dramatic inconsistencies. When Rochester takes Jane into his arms at the end, Herrmann rises into a full aria, replete with crashing cymbals (Herrmann said it was this score which led him to write his opera based on *Wuthering Heights*). Truffaut has commented, 'They often speak of Orson Welles as a poet; I see him rather as a musician. His Falstaff film *Chimes at Midnight* is the film which most resembles an opera. Orson Welles's work is prose which becomes music on the cutting bench. His films are shot by an exhibitionist and edited by a censor.' *Jane Eyre* suffers primarily because it lacks this musical unity, the 'interior conception' of an author.

The Stranger

André Bazin speaks of *The Stranger* as a 'parody' of a Welles film, and the remark is judicious. The story itself has the elements of a good film – an ex-Nazi teaching at a prep school in a small Connecticut town is hunted down by a war crimes investigator – but the writing, particularly in regard to the Nazi's wife, lapses into the merely implausible, and Welles's acting into the ridiculous. One critic's claim that we should not consider it a Welles film because he had little to do with writing it strikes me as a half-truth. Think of Edward G. Robinson (the investigator) playing the Welles role and vice versa, and there immediately arise tensions in the story which Welles fails to bring out. *The Stranger* might have been exciting if Robinson, who is adept at being simultaneously avuncular and sinister, had been able to show the Nazi gradually progressing from quietude to desperation as the investigator (Welles might have made the figure more ambiguous, and the original casting – Agnes Moorehead! – was more promising still) prods him to reveal himself. Certainly Welles was under a great handicap in having to work from a mediocre script, but the fact is that his direction, apart from the baroque opening pursuit and a few virtuoso long takes, is not much more than competent. The pointless proliferation of close-ups as the film heads towards its climax is ample evidence that Welles was losing any grip he might have had on the story.

'*The Stranger* is the worst of my films,' Welles admits. 'There is

The Stranger: Konstantin Shayne, Edward G. Robinson, Billy House

nothing of me in that picture. I did it to prove that I could put out a movie as well as anyone else. It is absolutely of no interest to me. I did not make it with cynicism, however. I did my best with it ... The best stuff in the picture was a couple of reels taking place in South America. [Producer Sam] Spiegel cut it entirely ... the only little things about the film I really like are the comments on the town, the drugstore man, details of this kind.'

The story has a close resemblance to the general pattern of Welles's films: the guilty secret, the nemesis/investigator, the scenes of unmasking, the chastened 'innocents', and the grand finale in which the Nazi falls from a church tower after being impaled on the sword of a clock figure. Just as plain, though, is the pointlessness – because of the lack of coherent realization – of the plot conflict. Any drama inherent in the wife's gradual awakening to her husband's past is destroyed, despite Loretta Young's good performance, by Welles's manic face-pulling and sinister muttering. The hero's 'secret' becomes a ludicrous joke at the expense of the rest of the world, for it is impossible to conceive of the character passing undetected by anyone, let alone the woman who married him. And his obsession with the church clock, which he tinkers with at all hours of the night, is mere fetishism, but without any Buñuelian moral overtones.

The revelation is equally preposterous – a supposedly cautious man giving way to a speech about Jews and 'the fiery sword of Siegfried'. After that, he gets stranger and stranger. The film demonstrates conclusively that Welles cannot play a self-effacing character; it would be like having Mae West play a nun. Instead of a devious interplay between two powerful characters, with a Desdemona-like wife being pulled between them, all we have is a number of pleasant (if excessively gullible) people watching a madman cavort and do tricks.

Odd Excursions

Welles has been able to keep his directorial hand in during periods of economic struggle by helping with the direction of numerous films in which he appears as an actor. Not obstreperously so, however; young directors who employ him find that he can be surprisingly docile about following orders. Maybe it's that he can't wait to get back to his own projects – he says that he doesn't particularly like to act, except in an occasional ambitious role such as Harry Lime or Falstaff, but does it because of the pleasure of being part of a film and because he needs the money. 'I am a fruit picker,' he once said. 'You go where the work is.' Occasionally, though, sympathetic or merely complaisant directors give him the chance to choose a few set-ups, rewrite dialogue, add bits of business. Indeed, it is hard to conceive of Welles restraining himself from making suggestions, and harder still to picture a director refusing to consider them. Even in his appearances on television variety shows there are tell-tale moments. He contrived to steal the ending of a television tribute to Mike Todd by thanking the audience for its forbearance, giving a moody furrow to his brow, and letting the camera hold on his massive opera-caped figure lumbering slowly away. He has even stolen the show from God – when he narrated Nicholas Ray's *King of Kings* and persisted in pronouncing the 't' in 'apostles'.

There is nothing worth remarking – or seeing – in such frankly silly romps as *Marco the Magnificent!*, *Is Paris Burning?*, *Casino Royale*, and the like. But there are considerable imprints of Welles in

Eddie Sutherland's *Follow the Boys* (1944), a troop-entertaining revue which re-creates with splendid panache a 'Mercury Wonder Show', Welles materializing out of a rabbit, levitating his cigar, sawing Marlene Dietrich in half and letting the lower part of her body prance about the stage; in Gregory Ratoff's *Black Magic* (1947), the story of the sorcerer Cagliostro, full of lugubrious trickery if uncohesive as a whole; most famously as the black-marketeer Harry Lime in Carol Reed's *The Third Man* (1949), a small but indelible part notable for the 'cuckoo clock' speech, which he wrote, and the sewer chase, which points towards his use of architectural monstrosities in *The Trial*; Hilton Edwards's *Return to Glennascaul* (1951), a charming little ghost story which begins with the master rehearsing *Othello* and follows him on a strange drive through the Irish countryside; John Huston's *Moby Dick* (1956), which Welles wanted to direct, settling instead on a splendiferous delivery of Father Mapple's whaling sermon; Richard Fleischer's *Compulsion* (1959), another ideal Welles subject which comes to life only when, as Clarence Darrow, he gives an impassioned plea for mercy towards the two cold young killers – a strange characterization, too, Welles playing the advocate as a man obsessed with the idea of murder; and *A Man for All Seasons* (1966), the brooding presence of Welles's Cardinal Wolsey challenging briefly the self-righteousness of the hero, and mysterious demonic flashes brightening the *mise-en-scène*.

Though the *œuvre* of Welles is small – thirteen completed feature films in thirty years – he has seldom been confined to idleness. He remained sporadically active in radio until 1953, in theatre until 1960, and has found television a congenial means of experiment, directing BBC 'sketchbooks'; a documentary on the Actors' Studio, *The Method*; *The Fountain of Youth*, a Peabody Award-winning adaptation of a John Collier short story; Italian television films; and, most recently, a CBS special, *Around the World with Orson Welles*, featuring a shortened version of *The Merchant of Venice*, with himself as Shylock.

One happy, if mysterious, offshoot of his dabbling in television was a half-hour adaptation of *Don Quixote*, begun in 1955, which grew into a feature film which is still uncompleted, apparently because Welles cannot think of an ending (how can the modern world, in which the film is set, tolerate Quixote's existence, he wonders, but how too could Quixote ever cease to exist?) and because he feels that it will be 'an execrated film' and he needs 'a big success' before putting it in circulation.

A Mexican critic, Humberto Arenal, found in 1957 that Welles was then quite sure about an ending: 'The story starts in a hotel in Mexico City where Patty McCormack is playing while Welles reads Cervantes' novel; she asks him what he is reading and he tries to explain. Thence, a 'flashback' consisting of three episodes (each twenty-seven minutes in length) which re-create the most important sequences of the satire in a twentieth-century setting: Don Quixote assailing the screen in a movie house when he sees the film's villain attack the heroine; defending the bull against the picador's onslaughts in a bullfight; driving Rosinante against the 'windmills' – in this case, a power shovel.

'The last episode ends with a nuclear explosion which annihilates our civilization . . . but from the ruins there emerge the haughty Knight and his obese shield-bearer, Sancho Panza – symbols of the indestructibility of noble ideas . . . Besides Miss McCormack, who plays Dulcinea, Welles used Akim Tamiroff in the part of Sancho Panza, and for the title role, Francisco Reiguera, a naturalized Mexican originally from Spain, who has been working in films in France, Italy, and the United States since 1913.'

It has been reported that Señor Reiguera, after the production had dragged on for five years or so, began sending telegrams to Welles imploring him to hurry up and finish *Don Quixote* so that he could take the leisure to die. Welles finally complied, shooting enough footage so that the film could be finished without the elderly gentleman.

7: The Lady From Shanghai

After several meandering years, Welles at last hit his stride again with *The Lady from Shanghai*, which remains his most purely enjoyable film. There is a new freedom of visual style, a willingness to relax, to accommodate *longueurs* and exhilarating bits of simple fun. In no other film, not even *Citizen Kane*, do we share with Welles such a spontaneous delight in the exercise of his gifts. There is no strain on the viewer, none of the ponderousness that will damage some of Welles's later films. The story is handled in a most cavalier fashion; indeed, it took me eight viewings to detach myself enough to figure out the plot. If it had not been for some of the darker underlying ironies and twists of convention, *The Lady from Shanghai* might have been a popular success. Welles destroys a number of highly romantic myths in the denouement, but he satisfies many of our expectations along the way. Howard Hawks's *The Big Sleep*, with an even more bewildering narrative, was an enormous success in 1946, the year in which *Shanghai* was made, and the public might have been willing to accept Rita Hayworth as a murderess. However, Columbia was so horrified at what Welles had done to her image that it held up the film's release for two years and rushed her into several more conventional roles.

The result was that *The Lady from Shanghai* lost a fortune and marked Welles as anathema in Hollywood. For all its detrimental effect on his credit with producers, though, Welles's devil-may-care attitude towards the plot is one of the foremost pleasures of the film. If we do not feel the great compression and exactness of execution that mark *Kane* and *The Ambersons* as masterpieces, we can see in the film's unforced pleasantness its superiority to a more pretentious work such as *The Trial*, not only as entertainment but also as a complex and effective expression of Welles's most deeply felt themes. As Robin Wood remarks of Hitchcock's *North by Northwest*: 'A light entertainment can have depth, subtlety, finesse, it can embody mature moral values; indeed it seems to me that it *must* . . . The tongue-in-cheek element on plot level has the function of directing our attention to other levels.'

Comparison with Hitchcock is inevitable, and as a simple thriller Welles's film has the same elements of irrationality and moral irony that confound critics who see Hitchcock as a mere manipulator of plot crises. In dealing with *The Lady from Shanghai*, the critic has a less onerous task in demonstrating the artist's seriousness, since Welles deals explicitly with themes which Hitchcock treats by implication – i.e. moral conflict within the law (which we see in *North by Northwest* as the government's callous use of a lady agent for sexual blackmail, but here as the revengeful trickery of a crippled lawyer), and transference of guilt (implicit in the total lack of justification for Cary Grant's abduction, and surreally explicit here in Grisby's plan to make O'Hara confess to a murder he did not commit).

The problem in discussing Welles's film will be to understand the ironic tension between the moral issues and the characters' apparent lack of interest in them. K.'s whole life in *The Trial* is changed by his investigation into the principles behind his case, and Quinlan in *Touch of Evil* spends most of his time rectifying the moral inadequacy of the law; but in *The Lady from Shanghai* O'Hara treats his legal predicament as only an unpleasant adventure which he must get through so that he can move on to a more important concern – Elsa Bannister, the lawyer's wife. Unfortunately, as he discovers, she is the instigator of the whole complex murder plot, and the issues encroach heavily on his fate despite his avoidance of them. At the end he has been forced to formulate a philosophical position which is similar to the tragic understanding which Welles's other heroes achieve, but of a less definitive nature. It is less a conclusion than a beginning, a coming to terms with the world.

The Lady from Shanghai, alone of Welles's works, is essentially a comedy. In *Chimes at Midnight*, Welles focuses on another innocent adventurer, but the qualities of resilience, open-heartedness and humour which allowed the young O'Hara to survive his disillusionment have now become the downfall of Falstaff, a tragic hero whose candour, like Othello's trustfulness, is his flaw. Michael O'Hara is a young Irish sailor (rather whimsically incarnated by Welles) who has been 'travelling around the world too much to find out anything about it' – Bannister's words and a fair statement of the dangers of moral blindness and idealistic gullibility which all of Welles's heroes face. Like the ignoble Van Stratten in *Mr Arkadin*, he will try anything once, but unlike Van Stratten, he is not out merely for money. He killed a man once, but it was for the Republicans in the Spanish Civil War, a salve for his self-esteem until Bannister's associate George Grisby (a breathtakingly funny and unnerving performance by Glenn Anders) tells him that killing during a war must not be murder. O'Hara's naïveté is as touching as it is farcical; he seems to be drawn to the most unsavoury, cunning characters as if by a universal design of which he is blithely unaware. He meets the beautiful Elsa and saves her from a mugging in Central Park, and with jaunty humility (which allows him to disclaim any moral identity), tells us, 'I start out in this story a little like a hero – which I most certainly am not.'

Soon after the lady contrives to have her husband, Arthur Bannister – memorably played by Everett Sloane – hire O'Hara as bosun of their yacht for a lengthy 'pleasure' cruise. At this point Grisby arrives to offer O'Hara a strange proposition, and the film becomes madly confusing. Harry Cohn, the producer, stomped out of a preview shouting, 'I'll give a thousand dollars to anyone who can explain the story to me!' Lucidity is not one of the film's virtues; an explication of the plot might help. Grisby will give O'Hara $5,000 to confess to killing him, so that he can disappear to a South Sea island, taking with him the insurance his wife will collect for him. Since there will be no body, O'Hara will not be convicted, but since there will be a confession, Grisby will be legally dead. Grisby will then spend his declining years far from the nuclear holocaust that he knows is coming. O'Hara goes along with the scheme uncomprehendingly, hoping to use the money to lure Elsa from her husband (the height of naïveté). On the night of the fake murder, Grisby shoots a divorce detective who has been hired by Bannister and who has discovered the truth of the plot. Just after Grisby has vanished, the dying detective tells O'Hara that he has

The Lady from Shanghai: the hall of mirrors (Welles, Rita Hayworth, Everett ▶
Sloane)

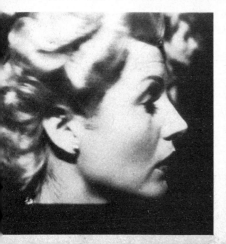

been framed, and that Grisby, with Elsa's help, is going to kill Bannister for his money and let Michael take the fall. O'Hara dashes to Bannister's office to prevent the murder, but is greeted by a horde of cops who find the confession in his pocket, and by Elsa and Bannister – and Grisby's corpse.

At this point O'Hara muses, 'either me or the rest of the whole world is absolutely insane' – the subtle temptation that also encourages Joseph K. to surrender. Bannister, who has never lost a case, defends O'Hara in a bitterly comic courtroom sequence, but intends to see him convicted. Just before the verdict is given, O'Hara manages to escape from the courthouse by feigning a suicide attempt and posing as a jury-man from another trial. He wanders into a theatre in Chinatown, followed by Elsa; her servants arrive and hustle him into the crazy house of an empty amusement park. After falling through a vertiginous series of traps and chutes that is a kind of apocalyptic vision of the chaos which awaits his surrender, he winds up in the hall of mirrors, where he is confronted with the endless reflections of his temptress's face. Bannister arrives and tells her that he has explained everything in a note to the district attorney (she killed Grisby because he had lost his head and shot the detective). The husband and wife shoot each other, the mirrors shattering all around them as O'Hara watches. She crawls out of the room, telling O'Hara that he shouldn't try to fight the evil of the world. He leaves her to die. As he walks off into the grey early morning, towards the sea, he tells us, 'I went to call the cops but I knew she'd be dead before they got there – I'd be free. Bannister's note to the D.A. fixed it, I'd be innocent officially. But that's a big word, "innocent" – stupid's more like it. Well – everybody is somebody's fool. The only way to stay out of trouble is to grow old, so I guess I'll concentrate on that. Maybe I'll live so long that I'll forget her – maybe I'll die trying.'

Welles explains the plot to us while he is wandering through the crazy house, and it is impossible to pay attention to what he is saying. The only thing we can be sure of (unless we have analysed the plot in repose) is that Elsa was the cause of it all, Bannister her reluctant protector, and O'Hara the intended victim. Grisby remains an absolute befuddlement. If we can't quite understand what makes him so afraid of the bomb (a common fear but improbable for him, since he seems as invulnerable as Iago until that marvellous moment when his corpse is wheeled past the astonished O'Hara, and the film pirouettes from irrationality into madness), neither can we see a plausible explanation – but for poetic compulsion – for the insouciant humour with which he dupes O'Hara. If the actor had not given such a brilliant, concrete, amusing performance – if the role had been played straight – Grisby might be too abstracted to shake us as much as he does. He would be as repellently sententious as the Advocate in *The Trial*. It is because of his three-dimensionality, paradoxically, that Grisby becomes a poetic force, a Fury wholly dedicated to exposing chaos and evil to the innocent O'Hara.

Bannister's nihilism repels O'Hara, but Elsa offers a subtler temptation – the lure of romantic fatalism. 'Everything's bad, Michael,' she tells him as they dance. 'Everything. You can't escape it or fight it. You've got to get along with it, deal with it, make terms.' Surrender is the ultimate evil, the ultimate indignity, in Welles's world, and what Elsa formulates, Bannister and Grisby demonstrate. As in the ending of *The Trial*, the bomb is the character's all-serving excuse for irresponsibility. Michelangelo Antonioni's celebrated statement that 'Under the bomb everyone is a hero, and under the bomb no one is a hero' finds its reply in O'Hara's accusation of Elsa: 'You mean we can't win? Then we can't lose either. Only if we quit.' Welles places his heroes *in extremis* to force them to define themselves, to make them fight or give up. He refuses to blame the universe at large for man's failings, realizing that such a feeling is sentimental at best and suicidal at worst. He surrounds the hero with people who have given in to irresponsibility or self-indulgent hysteria. Elsa needs security so desperately that she has succumbed to Bannister's economic blackmail; murder, self-destruction, is her only way out. We can only pity Bannister's acknowledgement of impotence. Grisby has the dignity of a psychotic who rules his own world with its own laws – like Quinlan in his abuse of legal technicalities, but unlike Quinlan in that his purposes are purely self-serving and self-denying. Grisby does not have tragic stature because there is no moral urgency to his actions. If he still attains Shakespearean comic proportions, it is because he revels in his (avowed) despair to such a degree that we would gladly follow him, were it not for the presence of a greater figure, for Welles's insistence on man's ability to transcend the folly around him.

The Lady from Shanghai: chaos in the court

It is significant that Welles should give to a beautiful woman, his former wife, the most precise formulation of his ultimate sin. Welles names the Bannister yacht 'The Circe', and has Elsa sing a song called 'Please Don't Kiss Me', which lures the spellbound O'Hara from the depths of the ship. O'Hara's tale of the blood-maddened sharks eating at their own flesh, the exotic haze of Chinatown, the chaotic fun-house with its signs reading 'Stand Up Or Give Up' and the dragon's jaws which swallow O'Hara, the furtive love-making before writhing sea-monsters in an aquarium, and the symbolic intercutting of the river picnic (Elsa with flamingo and snake, O'Hara with parrots, Grisby with crocodile) continually reinforce the romantic fascination of the lady's siren-like lure of the young sailor adrift in a world of sudden, bewildering dangers. The temptation offered by women in Welles's world is that of passivity, of sentimental and distracting reassurance, of a sheltering from reality which can become crippling. Mrs Kane's sled, Isabel's selfless devotion, Desdemona's purity, Raina's innocence, Doll Tearsheet's 'flattering busses' – all these are touching evocations of a vanished

The Lady from Shanghai: the yacht 'Circe'

past to which the hero may return for a vision of the alternative to the mania of power, but from which he must divorce himself lest he use its simplicity obsessively, blindly, as a talisman against evil.

O'Hara takes refuge from the malevolence of Bannister and Grisby in his image of Elsa, refusing to see that her complicity with evil has made her unspoiled loveliness all the more deadly for its dissimulation. She could truly say, 'I am not what I am.' At the end, the romanticist leaves his ideal to die – one of the most harrowing scenes Welles has given us, and the signal of that sombre disquiet which will for ever follow his mature heroes. When he returns to the man of good will twenty years later, that man is old, gross and moribund. His gaiety is haunted by melancholy, and his youthful spirit is a mockery of himself.

8: Macbeth and Othello

Welles and Shakespeare

Back in the days of the Mercury Theatre, John Houseman was asked when Welles's production of *Julius Caesar* would open. 'When Welles finishes writing it,' he replied. The feeling that Welles hurls himself against Shakespeare merely to gratify himself with the sound of the collision is as common as it is misleading. This assumption arises in part from the boisterous, uneven quality of some of Welles's adaptations and from the bravura aspects of his style, but it fails to take into account the common source of both the imperfections and the achievements. Shakespeare was Welles's first dramatic love, and whenever he has wanted to find himself artistically he has returned to Shakespeare's plays. In them he finds not only themes compatible with his own and characters large enough to justify his most grandiose conceptions but also a standard against which he can measure his own egotism, a theatrical ideal which challenges him to reconcile his subjective obsessions with the demands of universality.

Welles has refused to dramatize *Crime and Punishment*, explaining that he finds himself in complete agreement with Dostoevsky and would not be content just to illustrate the book. In Shakespeare, however, he finds a superior power whose dramas are capable of broadening, not merely confirming, his own ideas. When he adapts Shakespeare he is able to enlarge his conception of the hero without, as in *Mr Arkadin*, limiting his social perspective in the process. 'Shakespeare is the staff of life,' he has declared, and it is clear that Welles sees Shakespeare as his artistic conscience, the consummate

Welles as Othello

example of the fusion of a personal vision with the full complexity of human nature. If, like Shakespeare, he refuses to judge his characters and never violates his conception of character to make an ideological point, he also, like Shakespeare, at every point makes clear the precise moral structure under which his characters live. In Shakespeare also he is able to find an appropriate setting for his kingly characters to inhabit. Just as John Ford leaves the unheroic present for the American frontier, Welles finds in medieval castles and battlefields a setting congenial to true grandeur of spirit. In *Touch of Evil* and *Citizen Kane*, he is able to create fittingly heroic universes for his heroes to rule, but in *Mr Arkadin* and *The Trial* the moral smallness of the heroes collides with Welles's attempts to conjure up an egocentric universe. The Shakespearean form, however, minimizes such dangers by allowing Welles freely to allocate to a Macbeth, an Othello, and a Falstaff social power which would be difficult to justify in a less feudal world.

As a young man, Welles approached his master with boundless ego. He staged an all-black production of *Macbeth* in Harlem, turning the witches into voodoo doctors and changing the locale to Haiti; he played *Caesar* in modern dress as an allegory of fascism; and, most spectacularly, he combined eight of Shakespeare's history plays into a monstrous spectacle called *Five Kings*, which sealed the

107

doom of the Mercury Theatre. His three Shakespearean films have been more and more faithful to the letter of Shakespeare but, paradoxically, less and less faithful to the spirit as he acquires more grace and confidence in uniting Shakespeare's vision to his own. If Welles no longer pulls a stunt like the voodoo *Macbeth*, he takes a larger, subtler liberty in changing the emphasis of the Falstaff–Hal story from the moral awakening of the ideal king to the wilful destruction of innocence by a young man newly conscious of power. Welles's theme was there all the time, of course, and the kingship theme is as subsidiary to Welles as it is paramount to Shakespeare. The point is that Welles's vision has finally matured, so that we no longer feel the damaging pull between one moral system and another, as we do, for example, in his *Othello*, in which both the text and Welles's acting resist his inchoate attempt to make Iago the hero. What Welles has conquered is the diffusion of emphasis and statement, so that he no longer tries to tell the entire history of England from 1377 to 1485, but concentrates instead on the moral drama behind the story of a single king. The audience of *Chimes at Midnight* is scarcely aware of the extensive textual revision and rearranging that Welles has unobtrusively performed on the plays; for *Five Kings* that was one of the central fascinations.

A Welles adaptation of Shakespeare is not an *ad hoc* project but the result of a lifetime of scholarship and creative experiment. The genesis of *Chimes at Midnight*, for example, extends even beyond *Five Kings*. Welles had written a first adaptation of the chronicles when he was twelve years old and a student at the Todd School in Woodstock – where he was director of a student company that performed not only Shakespeare but also other Elizabethan playwrights such as Jonson, Marlowe, Dekker, and Ford. The project incubated until Welles staged *Chimes at Midnight* in Belfast in 1960; he was finally able to raise money for the film in 1964, and completed it in 1966 after almost forty years of contemplation and experimentation.

Shakespeare has been his touchstone for nearly his entire life. As he tells it, his mother had read him Lamb's *Tales from Shakespeare* when he was two, and when he discovered that they were not the real thing but had been watered down for children, he demanded that she read him the plays themselves. She gave him his first book, *A Midsummer Night's Dream*, for his third birthday, and he quickly began to assemble the complete works of Shakespeare in his library. He attended productions of the plays from an early age, and directed his own adaptations of Shakespeare (as well as his own plays) in his puppet theatre for his family, supplying all the voices himself. By the time he was seven he could recite any speech from *King Lear*, and by the time he was ten, he claims, he had learned all the tragic parts. At the age of nine, he had played Lear in a condensed version in his back yard. He delighted in playing the great monsters – Richard III, Brutus (and Cassius in the same production), Scrooge, Judas. He proved his versatility by playing the Blessed Virgin in one play, Christ in another. When he was a teenager he declared that Webster's *The Duchess of Malfi* was his favourite play, though as he has grown older he has proved more partial to *Lear*, which he still hopes to film.

Leni Riefenstahl has made an interesting comment on Welles's Shakespearean films: 'Orson Welles draws marvellous pictures in the margin of Shakespeare, but his films are like operas or ballets suggested by Shakespeare, not Shakespeare himself.' Welles's position is similar: 'I use Shakespeare's words and characters to make motion pictures. They are variations on his themes . . . Without presuming to compare myself to Verdi, I think he gives me my best justification. The opera *Otello* is certainly not *Othello* the play. It certainly could not have been written without Shakespeare, but it is first and foremost an opera. *Othello* the movie, I hope, is first and foremost a motion picture.' If Welles changes Shakespeare's emphasis to ally it more closely to his own, his intention is not to distort, attack, or ignore the text. The problem he explores in *Macbeth* and *Othello* and brings to fruition in *Chimes at Midnight* is primarily one of integration and stylization. The two early films are seriously handicapped, *Macbeth* by extreme budgetary restrictions and a resulting crudeness of tone (which in some ways, however, helps to create the necessary atmosphere of monolithic superstition, though it hinders Welles in smoothly integrating his concept of Macbeth's character with Shakespeare's), and *Othello* by inadequate sound synchronization (which necessitates some evasive camerawork and blurs the impact of much of the dialogue), and by the problem of reconciling Iago to the text.

But most vital to Welles's concerns, and resolved partially in *Othello*, is the question of striking a stylistic balance between poetry

Macbeth: Macbeth and Banquo in the fog

and setting. *Macbeth* is performed in papier-maché sets, and only in the foggy exteriors do we find the necessary naturalistic counterpoint. For *Othello*, Welles was able to shoot his exteriors in Italy, Morocco, and on the island of Torcello, and the resulting freedom in selection of settings adds immensely to the mood. The scene of Duncan's arrival in *Macbeth*, for example, cannot, for all its details of pagan drummers and horrific costumes, avoid the distracting appearance of a sound-stage with painted backdrop for sky, constructed rocks, and so forth. We are thrown back on our sense of the drama as a theatrical spectacle, and Welles's style is too expressionistic to accommodate such totally unreal surroundings without disturbing the ironic tension he requires between the hero's overweening ego and the constraints of social responsibility. The miniature long-shots of the castle in *Citizen Kane* work well because Welles juxtaposes them in the newsreel with documentary shots of the actual Hearst castle; since we have already seen aerial views of the castle in the daylight, we can easily accept the stylization of the darkened castle seen through hazy trees with tiny lights flickering here and there in the gloom. The tension of setting is perfectly allied with that of character: as Kane retreats deeper and deeper into a self-enclosed fantasy world, we no longer see the castle as a real object but as a projection of his imagination. Similarly, Welles takes great pains in the early parts of *The Ambersons* to establish the documentary verity of the mansion and the town surrounding it; as the mood becomes more claustrophobic, we see less of the total view and more of the expressionistically shadowed and distorted interiors.

We can conclude that the more stylized the Wellesian character, the more carefully considered must be the deployment of landscape and setting. If the settings of *Macbeth* make such considerations impossible, and drive the work into pure expressionism with its attendant virtues and limitations, the settings of *Chimes at Midnight* solve the problem brilliantly. First of all, Welles filmed in Spain – not merely because Spanish money was behind the production but because in the Moorish castles, towns and faces, he could find a world which, like the hellish border setting of *Touch of Evil*, is not slavishly literal and historical but permits any latitude of shading from the naturalistic to the grotesque. We see this too in *Othello*, perhaps most clearly in the scene on the parapet in which Iago goads Othello's jealousy. The photography is that of an eerie, slightly unreal twilight. Othello wears a massive white robe, light from the left casting a hazy aura on his profile; he strides back and forth, driving Iago closer and closer to the edge of the precipice below which, from a dizzying height, we see waves smashing. Kurosawa achieved a similar stylization in the forest scenes of *Throne of Blood*, his version of *Macbeth*, in which the two men on horses wheel around violently in the throes of a wild thunderstorm, their movements foreshortened and made more spasmodic by the compressed perspective of a long-focus lens.

The problem of a world-style has been solved in Westerns and in Japanese period pictures, Welles explains, because of the long evolution of a tradition. With Shakespeare, as he puts it, 'These are people who have more life in them than any human being ever had. But you can't simply dress up and *be* them, you have to make a world for them . . . In *Henry V*, for example, you see the people riding out of the castle, and suddenly they are on a golf course somewhere charging each other. You can't escape it, they have entered another world . . . What I am trying to do is to see the outside, real world through the same eyes as the inside, fabricated one. To create a kind of unity.' Welles is raising here the problem of *mise-en-scène*, of the integration of character and poetry with visual rhythm, which will be our particular concern in discussing his three Shakespearean films.

Macbeth

Throughout his sojourn in Hollywood, Welles tried, vainly, to interest the major companies in a plan to film *Macbeth* with sparse settings and with all the acting and camerawork rehearsed in advance. Finally he persuaded Herbert Yates, the president of Republic Pictures, the adventurous and much-maligned quickie studio, to finance him. Yates had admired Welles's previous work and was impressed by his promise to shoot the film in three weeks. For rehearsal Welles took his cast (which then included Agnes Moorehead as Lady Macbeth) to the Utah Centennial Festival in Salt Lake City. He then went to Hollywood and finished the film in twenty-three days, for less than $200,000. *Macbeth* evoked wide derision because of its refusal to indulge, however hastily, in conventional niceties.

Our first appeal is not to authority – an ignoble word when confronted with such recalcitrance – but to friendly understanding. Jean Cocteau, who found the black *Macbeth* a 'strange and magnificent spectacle', had this to say about the film after Welles showed it to him in a little room in Venice: 'Orson Welles's *Macbeth* leaves the spectator deaf and blind, and I truly believe that the people who like it (among whom I am proud to include myself) expect this . . . Coiffed with horns and crowns of cardboard, clad in animal skins like the first motorists, the heroes of the drama move in the corridors of a kind of dream underground, in devastated caves leaking water, in an abandoned coal-mine. The shots are always hazardous. The camera is always found where the eye of destiny follows his victims. At times we ask ourselves in what age this nightmare is taking place, and when we encounter Lady Macbeth for the first time before the camera moves back and places her, we almost see a lady in modern dress lying on a fur couch next to the telephone.

'In the role of Macbeth, Orson Welles offers us a considerable tragedian, and if the Scottish accent imitated by the Americans is perhaps unbearable to English ears, I find that it does not disturb me and that even if I perfectly possessed the English language, I would not be disturbed, because this is what one can expect from these bizarre monsters who express in a monstrous language the words of

Macbeth: 'like the first motorists . . .' Welles as Macbeth

Shakespeare, which remain their words. In brief, I am a poor judge and a better judge than another in the sense that, without the least disturbance, I only take part in the plot, and my malaise comes only from that rather than from a fault of accent.'

The lack of any sense of the hero's moral relationship to society – intensified by the play's supernatural aspects and by the hallucinatory, almost solipsistic nature of Macbeth's ambition, which is too compulsive to admit of rational calculation – turns the drama farther inward than in any Welles film until *The Immortal Story*. We are in a theatre of the subconscious. We are led, however, not into Macbeth's superego but into his id. At its most effective, *Macbeth* resembles classic horror films such as *El* and *King Kong* (one of Welles's favourite films), dramas which avoid nuance of character in order to more effectively present the clash of extreme emotions and actions and free us into the world of nightmare. *Macbeth* falters when the camera merely observes the characters giving speeches. The implicit emotional complexity of the words, which the actors (except for Dan O'Herlihy as Macduff) quite simply ignore, serves only to distract us from the directness of the images; in a nightmare we do not pause for contemplation, but are swept along helplessly, uncritically. There is no subtlety in Welles's playing of Macbeth. If his performance, though it is scarcely more than adequate, strikes us as more appropriate than his Othello, which he plays in a similarly transfixed, manic way, it is because the *mise-en-scène* calculates along such raw, direct lines. Welles employs many long takes, but for budgetary reasons moves his actors much more than he moves his camera; usually we see Macbeth pivoting around in the extreme foreground and the other characters gravitating towards him from the distance. *Macbeth* is marked also by an overwhelming concentration on close-ups; again, partly a result of haste and desperation, but also a prime factor in demonstrating the amoral egocentricity of the hero.

Macbeth is even more nightmarish than *The Trial*, because we do not watch from an ironic distance. We are thrust without explanation or qualification into fear and chaos. To say that the film falls into the realm of melodrama rather than that of tragedy is not as damning as it may seem. Welles has accepted the imposed limitations and has quite boldly shaped them to his own ends. What appals Macbeth, A. C. Bradley has commented, 'is always the image of his own guilty heart or bloody deed, or some image which derives from them its terror or gloom. These, when they arise, hold him spellbound and possess him wholly, like a hypnotic trance which is at the same time the ecstasy of a poet ... His imagination is ... something usually deeper and higher than his conscious thoughts; and if he had obeyed it he would have been safe.' Welles's Macbeth is the centre of a whirlwind of destructive activity which evokes less a struggle of the will for dominance than a struggle of the mind for consciousness. The change in him after the murder is almost indistinguishable; he seems to be sleepwalking from the beginning, and his blindness to the possibility of free choice makes it difficult for us to consider him a tragic hero.

The witches in Shakespeare merely prophesy to Macbeth – there is nothing in the play, Bradley points out, that enables us to consider them the masters of his destiny – and their suggestions rouse forces of violence which he has long held in submission, directing them to the legitimate ends of warfare rather than towards illegitimate ambition. Welles makes of the witches something entirely different. In the opening sequence, which we have seen in almost every Welles film to be the indication of 'original sin' and the establishment of an ironic, godlike parenthesis to the hero's actions, the hands of the witches are seen moulding a clay figure in their boiling pot, shaping

Macbeth: the priest in braids (Alan Napier)

it into the likeness of a child and placing a crown on its head. The witches carry pronged druidical staffs, and stand on a hill when Macbeth first meets them. The last shot of the film shows them standing with their staffs in the fog swirling around Macbeth's castle, strikingly reminiscent of *Kane*.

Welles also creates a new character, a tall, forbidding priest in long braids who leads Duncan and his court in an incantation (actually a common Catholic prayer) to renounce Satan 'and the other evil spirits who roam about the world seeking the destruction of souls'. The final appearance of the 'voodoo' Macbeth comes at the moment when Macduff swings his sword at Macbeth's neck. Welles cuts to the clay figure – its head is cut off, the tiny crown falls to the ground; and Macduff hurls Macbeth's head from the promontory. The feeling is of an inchoate society vacillating dangerously between paganism and a rudimentary Christian ethic. Macbeth is torn between these contradictions without being able to articulate them beyond his realization that:

> ... this Duncan
> Hath borne his faculties so meek, hath been
> So clear in his great office, that his virtues
> Will plead like angels, trumpet-tongued, against
> The deep damnation of his taking-off ...

Duncan is thus the prototype of the Christian king, of whom Welles will have more to say in *Chimes at Midnight*, but he is so only in Macbeth's conscience; even less than in Shakespeare do we feel any sense of Duncan's power and nobility. Duncan does nothing in the film but preside over the renunciation of Satan and the peremptory execution of Macbeth's vanquished captive which immediately precedes it; his progress to court is preceded by a swarm of dogs and pigs. Macbeth kisses his lady with gibbeted corpses dangling in the background. Such a society can only encourage Macbeth's ambition.

Shakespeare would not make the witches agents of fate because his conception of character is closely allied to the notion of a great and inviolable order of nature, which Macbeth perceives (though dimly) in his soliloquies. Welles's concerns are with the conscience of the hero as a force reflecting on itself to the exclusion of society. No matter how venal the Welles hero, his struggle is paramount because there is no one else of equal stature; and, unlike in Shakespeare, the hero makes no recognition (until the moment of his destruction) of an order greater than himself. If the witches are to Shakespeare's Macbeth only a catalyst to his ambition, to Welles they are the very agents of Macbeth's destruction, the forces which have formed him and which he has not found the strength to surmount.

The factor which contributes most decisively to Macbeth's lack of moral reference is the weakness of Jeanette Nolan as Lady Macbeth. The sleepwalking scene should crystallize for Macbeth as well as for the audience the undercurrent of hideously repressed guilt that drives him to despair of salvation, but because of the actress the scene is an excruciating embarrassment which negates that understanding by making the expression of guilt even more intolerable than its denial. Macbeth is thus robbed of the tragic ambience granted to Welles's other heroes, and his struggle is merely pathetic. With Agnes Moorehead, the film no doubt would be immeasurably more successful; we can see in *The Lady from*

Shanghai how effectively Welles can describe the passage from seduction to madness, and in *The Ambersons* how the director and actress make recrimination and hysteria a moral counterpoint to the hero's slow movement from delusion to awareness. All we can see in Lady Macbeth here, however, is a fatal distraction. She is no creature of pity and terror, but a comfortingly mad figure in the background of Macbeth's consciousness. There is no sense that she means anything at all to him, and when he hears of her death and gives the 'Tomorrow, and tomorrow, and tomorrow' speech, Welles shows us not the anguished face of a moral partner but great rolling banks of fog – as if her death is not a vision of the folly of pride but the sublime temptation of a dream-like merging into the shadows of a dim, unformed existence.

Othello

'Strange sense of Eternity in relation to film of *Othello*,' is an entry in the amusing diary Welles's Iago, his old friend Micheál Mac-Liammóir, kept of the filming and published as *Put Money in Thy Purse*. None of the projects in Welles's chequered career, except perhaps the mysterious *Don Quixote*, better attests to his persistence in the face of monumental difficulties. The filming took the better part of four years, with Welles taking time out to raise money by acting in Henry King's *Prince of Foxes* and Henry Hathaway's *The Black Rose*, which he regarded as jokes, and in *The Third Man*. No space here to detail Welles's endless search for a Desdemona or his frantic attempts to cut corners and continually reassemble the cast from everywhere in Europe; once, for example, he spirited equipment from the set of *The Black Rose*, under cover of darkness, and hurriedly shot scenes for *Othello* while nobody was looking. MacLiammóir saw the cast as members of a 'chic but highly neurotic lumber camp'. The whole maniacal enterprise came to a head when Welles collapsed on the set. Complete rest was prescribed, but of course he was soon back at work.

Welles's heroism in completing the film makes criticism of the result seem almost churlish, but the fact remains that *Othello* as a story stubbornly resists much of Welles's moral framework, and his style, never more floridly expressionistic, is particularly unsuited for a character conflict which depends so much on careful, logical, introspective development. *Macbeth* shares this problem, though to

117

a lesser degree, because of Macbeth's comparatively simpler, more elemental conflict – Lady Macbeth is single-minded, but she has none of the devious subtlety of Iago. Welles places great weight on Iago in the early, formative scenes of *Othello*, showing Othello only in brief scenes of courting and military pomp; but when Othello's passion finally takes hold of him, Welles almost wholly excludes Iago from the action. Iago is primarily a catalyst in Shakespeare, too, but the emphasis in Shakespeare is less on the acting-out of Othello's passion than on the development of it. Welles would like the film to be about the tension between dormancy and power in Othello, it seems – he omits much of the intricacy of Iago's schemes, tending instead to cross-cut from Iago watching to Othello doing – but, with the deliberations scanted, the film teeters wildly into unrestrained grand opera.

Welles revels in what he tries to exorcize, much like Ingmar Bergman in his unbearably claustrophobic *Hour of the Wolf*, another story of the impingement of mind into matter. Instead of making us share in madness by carefully displacing normal emotions into an irrational context, as Bergman does in *The Shame* and Welles in *The Lady from Shanghai*, the films present mere spectacles of frenzy and disintegration – fascinating as spectacle but alienating as drama. *Othello* seems to be a veritable celebration of Welles's obsessions; we hunger for a spark of sanity. And Manny Farber's comment on Liv Ullmann in *Hour of the Wolf* – 'like a sharp knife going through old cheese' – could be applied to Suzanne Cloutier's Desdemona, a clear, forceful characterization as revivifying as a breath of nascent oxygen.

I hesitate to apply the word 'decadent' to any of Welles's work, facile damnation as it usually is and unheeding of the virtues of a style which has reasons for pushing past the limits of naturalism; but in comparison with a powerful (if confusing) narrative such as *The Lady from Shanghai*, *Othello* is self-absorbed and rhetorically diffuse – decadent indeed. Like Othello, Michael O'Hara is of a 'free and open nature', and is naïvely subject to the machinations of a superior, envious, and self-destructive intellect. But *Shanghai* is in a quite honest sense a comedy; we take a detached, morally qualified view of O'Hara's difficulties while at the same time sharing in his emotional compulsions. Welles's Othello might invite our derision, so anaesthetized he seems next to the clear-willed Iago, but Welles will not allow us to see anything but tragic nobility behind his actions. Granted that it is an almost insuperably difficult part, the hardest part Shakespeare ever wrote, according to Laurence Olivier, who dares, in Stuart Burge's filmed transcription of the play, to treat Othello as a flamboyant, swaggering, almost ludicrous innocent; still, Welles's admiration for Othello as the only character capable of action in a world of impotent observers dangerously circumvents any kind of qualification to his actions. When Desdemona is killed, we are shocked and horrified, but we are shocked at the enormity of the gesture, not by its injustice. As Othello, Welles conveys little real feeling aside from anger; the speech to the senate about his wooing of Desdemona is delivered in a flat manner which suggests that her attraction to him was inevitable – there is none of the sense of wonder which Olivier so simply conveys. Gone, too, is Othello's childlike 'My wife! My wife! What wife? I have no wife,' after the murder. Desdemona is merely an unfortunate victim, and her death is not so much a reproach to Othello's folly as a confirmation of his unreflected ability to act.

It is strange, too, to see Welles playing the 'innocent' in a drama of power and entrapment; this is the only time in his work, aside from *Shanghai*, in which he has assumed the role. In *Macbeth*, Lady Macbeth is almost irrelevant, and Macbeth is the true source of ambition. But here, for whatever bizarre reasons (not the least of which was the impossibility of asking another actor to spend four years in the central role), he plays the dupe. Perhaps at this stage in his career, Welles felt an urgent need to explore the freer, more adventurous side of his character; among his unrealized projects of the time was a film of *The Odyssey*. It is no accident, then, that Othello loses much of his tragic stature and that Iago becomes the most interesting character, if not the central character, in the drama.

Welles and MacLiammóir decided that sexual impotence would be the motive for Iago, and MacLiammóir gives a marvellous performance, using the effeminate Roderigo as his lackey (oddly, Welles himself dubs in Roderigo's voice) and lowering his eyes darkly when he sees Desdemona throw herself into Othello's arms. This emphasis is consistent with Welles's basic themes. The malign cripple Bannister uses O'Hara and his own wife in a similarly masochistic

Othello: Iago in his cage (Micheál MacLiammóir)

scheme, sexual impotence serving as a metaphor for moral perversion and the pathos of the character defining his lack of moral stature. Our first sight of Iago after the prologue is as he stands in the back of a church watching Othello's wedding, and his muttered imprecation 'I hate the Moor' immediately assumes connotations both of jealousy and of sacrilege. Welles makes much throughout of Othello's easy martial power, his implacable worldly confidence; phallic cannon blasts occur buoyantly as he kisses Desdemona and when he enters her bedchamber, and ironically after he shouts 'Cuckold me!' and when Iago says that he will use Cassio against Othello.

The full extent of Welles's fascination with Iago is revealed at the very onset, when Iago is dragged past the funeral procession of Othello and Desdemona and thrown into a cage, thence to be suspended and to ponder the depths of his malignity. The cage appears throughout the film – hanging outside the nuptial chamber! – and the emphasis given to it, like the emphasis on Iago at the beginning, is a reflection of his control of Othello at the expense of his own life. Welles usually reserves such metaphors for his hero. Even in *The Lady from Shanghai*, Bannister is introduced well after O'Hara, after we have been well prepared to see O'Hara as the central figure. But the beginning of *Othello* establishes a dual

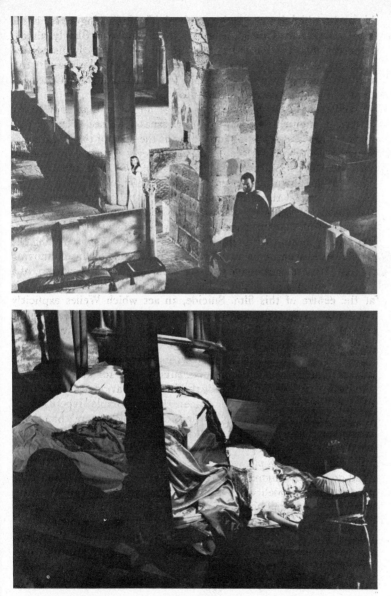

'. . . an overwhelming sense of vertigo' (Welles and Suzanne Cloutier)

hierarchy which is never quite resolved. The first thing we see in the film is the face of Othello, eyes closed, upside down. Slowly, almost imperceptibly, the image begins to move. We are eerily dissociated from any sense of time or space, and it is only when Welles cuts to a medium shot of a procession that we understand that Othello is dead and is being carried by pall-bearers.

Welles has used this startling image no fewer than four times, always in moments of acute powerlessness: we see O'Hara's face upside down and resolving into focus at the start of the crazy-house sequence, Joseph K.'s face upside down, eyes closed and resolving into focus as he awakes at the beginning of *The Trial*, and Wolsey's face upside down the moment before death in *A Man for All Seasons*. Several times in *Othello*, when Othello first succumbs to the throes of jealousy and when he reels around after stabbing himself, Welles creates an hallucinatory centrifugal motion by panning rapidly around with Othello from a very low angle, making the whole world seem to be swimming around behind his madly moving figure. These images convey an overwhelming sense of vertigo, of a world without a governing principle, and the surrender to chaos is at the centre of this film. Suicide, an act which Welles explicitly condemns in *The Trial*, is the only course open for a character as morally impotent as Othello, whose nobility is solely in the grandeur of his self-destruction.

If Welles is temperamentally wrong to play (and probably to direct) Othello – as he is temperamentally right for Falstaff, Caesar and Lear – this does not preclude the film from having many moments of spellbinding purity and grace: the inexorable repetition of the movement of Desdemona's veiled cortège; the camera's breathless movement towards Desdemona as she watches Othello address the senate; the mysterious shot of two mechanical bellringers sounding after Iago says 'I am not what I am'; the slow movement of Othello's hand down Desdemona's dress towards the rosary in her hand as he accuses her of infidelity; the chilling shot in which the camera moves away from Iago and his shadow follows Othello; the radiant appearance of Desdemona on her husband's return from sea, banners and heralds of his victory in shadow all around her; and the silent, astonished writhing of her face as Othello smothers her in the handkerchief. If the film as a whole is severely flawed, these moments are indeed as great as their antecedents in Shakespeare's verse.

9: Mr Arkadin

'And now I'm going to tell you about a scorpion. A scorpion wanted to cross a river, so he asked a frog to carry him. "No," said the frog. "No, thank you. If I let you on my back you may sting me, and the sting of the scorpion means death." "Now where," asked the scorpion, "is the logic of that? No scorpion could be judged illogical. If I sting you, you will die – I will drown." The frog was convinced and allowed the scorpion on his back, but just in the middle of the river he felt a terrible pain and realized that after all the scorpion *had* stung him. "Logic!" cried the dying frog, as he started under, bearing the scorpion down with him. "There is no logic in this!" "I know," said the scorpion, "but I can't help it – it's my character." Let's drink to character!'

Welles in Mr Arkadin

If *The Stranger* is self-parody, albeit unconscious, *Mr Arkadin* * is something more dangerous and more interesting: a work, like Sternberg's *The Devil is a Woman* or Ford's *Donovan's Reef*, in which the artist pushes his style past its limits, treating his most personal themes self-consciously, with a measure of irony, and in a manner not pretending to physical or psychological realism. The result, if successful, is a refinement of the artist's themes to a high pitch of intensity, an intoxicating liberation. The given story is kept purposefully simple so as not to hinder the free expression of character and motif. The pitfalls of such excess are obvious, though for Sternberg and Ford the problem is less acute because on a basic level the concerns of the director and the general audience coincide. Ford's audience can respond to Lee Marvin playing with toy trains without having to see in it a comic treatment of the primitive anarchism of Liberty Valance; Sternberg's audience can respond to the charms of Marlene Dietrich. But Welles pretends to no such level of common response, and in this we may see the essential failure of *Mr Arkadin*.

Thematically, Welles is returning to *Citizen Kane* from a more

---

* British title: *Confidential Report.*

disillusioned viewpoint. Gregory Arkadin is a legendary vizier of finance who lives in a fairytale castle, shepherding his daughter's waning innocence while brooding over the ruined lives he has left in his wake. A young man named Guy Van Stratten comes to Arkadin in search of possible fortune and is hired to reconstruct the fragments of his shadowed past, much as Thompson delves into Kane's life – but with the crucial difference that Arkadin is still alive, lending to the research a disturbing air of godlike detachment. Van Stratten finds out too much and frightens the old man by threatening to tell his daughter how her father made his fortune (white slavery). Arkadin flies to silence him, but on hearing that Van Stratten has told her the secret, jumps from his aeroplane without waiting to hear her response. Thompson's realization was that the life of even a legendary man is too complex to be rationalized away, but Van Stratten's conclusion is more cynical: he finds that by confronting legend with the truth, he can destroy the meaning of both.

We do not need the wretched performance of Robert Arden to see that Van Stratten is, in the words of a French critic, an 'uninteresting adventurer'. Only Raina Arkadin's stoical acceptance of her father's life and death allows us to consider an alternative to the madness of self-annihilation. Her equanimity, her sanity, her stance outside of judgement (well played by Paola Mori, Welles's wife) indicates that her love for Arkadin is more mature than Isabel's for George or Desdemona's for Othello. 'He was capable of anything,' she says simply, without sentimentality but with a kind of quiet awe and respect. The Welles hero has become an even more tragic figure; his plight seems more terrible when we reflect that his struggle for dignity is no longer a vital concern for those around him. It is a lonely self-examination in an arena peopled with impassive spectators. There is no Thompson to be chastened by the example; Raina accepts her father's actions as inevitable. *Touch of Evil* and *The Trial* will carry this bitterness even further, and not until *Chimes at Midnight* will we again find compassion after the end.

We are certainly not to see *Mr Arkadin* in terms of 'believable' characters and situations. Indeed, Arkadin's sole purpose is to obliterate the truth about himself and to vanish into the shadow of legend. We are back to the stylization of *Macbeth*, to the melodrama

124

Mr Arkadin: 'a variety of masks.'

of *The Stranger* without the pretext of naturalism. Arkadin's face is false to an unmistakable degree, and it would be absurd to criticize Welles for lack of 'subtlety' in make-up. This is as far from the point as criticizing Shakespeare for inadequately motivating Iago. Welles's nose has never before looked so fabricated, his costumes never so bizarre. He sports a variety of masks, and at one point dresses as Santa Claus! In several scenes we are permitted to see the backing which secures his wig, moustache and beard to his head.

All of which is to say that the theatricality of Arkadin's person is not a gaffe on Welles's part but the expression of the fear closest to his soul. Arkadin has no more desire to live when he can no longer hide the truth about himself from the one person he cares for, Raina. Welles's youthful idealism is reflected in Kane's attempt to preserve the spirit of his past by entombing himself, Pharaoh-like, with the relics of a happier existence. Arkadin, however, pleads that he has no memory prior to a night in 1927 when he found himself in Zürich with two hundred thousand Swiss francs in the pocket of his coat. He hires Van Stratten to discover the last remaining traces of his prior existence so that he can systematically obliterate them. He then plans to obliterate Van Stratten, by now the embodiment of his past, but failing to do so, must destroy himself. Lucidity is the ultimate crisis in Welles's universe. His heroes deceive themselves,

125

and destroy themselves at the moment when they can no longer hide their self-deception. Myth-making and iconoclasm are the two essential, irreconcilable poles of his personality. A crucial passage of dialogue sums up Arkadin's reasoning:

Arkadin: You are a dangerous man to be seen with.
Van Stratten: Yeah – I guess that's the way you had it planned all along.
Arkadin: I knew what I wanted – that's the difference between us. In this world there are those who give and those who ask, those who do not care to give, and those who do not dare to ask. You dared, but you were never quite sure what you were asking for. Now there's nothing more you can hope to win from me, Van Stratten. Not money – certainly not my daughter. Not even your life.

In keeping with the egocentricity that is Arkadin's sole *raison d'être*, the place he inhabits is no place in particular. The camera ranges all over the world, but what it sees is unreal. We see Arkadin standing immobile in the cabin of a wildly gyrating boat, but the boat has no destination. He gives a masked ball, but for no purpose other than to hide his face from Van Stratten until the hour of unmasking. This is reminiscent of a chillingly ironic scene in Chaplin's *The Idle Class*. The tramp wanders into a costume ball and is accepted by the partygoers because they think that he is masquerading as a tramp. The joke is on them. Arkadin, as mockingly solipsistic as Chaplin's tramp, merges silently with the crowd, cannily luring them into acknowledging that they too are hiding the secret of their natures. The crowd has no equivalent understanding. Arkadin is a mystery to Van Stratten not for moral or aesthetic reasons – as Kane is to Thompson – but because the key to the mystery is simply the key to money. Sex or love does not enter into his relationship with Raina; she is only a key to the key. A procession of religious *penitenti* outside the castle makes no more impression on him than the profane chaos of the party. Simple words of his narration whisk him here and there in a *rondo* of pointless frenzy.

Welles prefaces *Mr Arkadin* with a text explicitly stating his theme, which is also a theme of his work as a whole: 'A certain great and powerful king once asked a philosopher, "What can I give you of all that I have?" The man replied wisely, "Anything, sir, except your secret."' The problem with the film is that it treats a theme at the

Mr Arkadin: the masked ball

expense not only of character and dramatic logic but also of specific interest. We can accept Van Stratten as a one-dimensional foil and Arkadin as a philosophical proposition if we consider the work as a reflective commentary by Welles on the pattern of his career, but we cannot accept *Mr Arkadin* as an integral work. *The Old Man and the Sea* enables us to see with extraordinary clarity the elements of wish-fulfilment and ego-projection which underly all of Hemingway's work, but the basic anecdote of the story has been diluted by over-emphasis, so that the story is submerged by the weight of its component parts. *Mr Arkadin* is similarly self-indulgent.

In freeing himself of the burdens of naturalism, Welles also dissipated much of his underlying theme, so that we have no interest in Van Stratten and little respect for Arkadin. Though Welles demands of us that we find in Arkadin passion and nobility of purpose, the character is too abstracted to move us in a particular sense. Welles has said that 'the point of the story is to show that a man who declares himself in the face of the world, I am as I am, take it or leave it, that this man has a sort of tragic dignity. It is a question

Mr Arkadin: Robert Arden with (*above*) Akim Tamiroff and (*below*) Mischa Auer

of dignity, of verve, of courage, but it doesn't justify him ...
Arkadin created himself in a corrupted world; he doesn't try to
better that world, he is a prisoner of it.' Unfortunately, as with
Joseph K. in *The Trial*, we are forced to *will* Arkadin our understanding and sympathy, and the effort breaks the back of the work.
When Welles tells us at the outset that Arkadin's suicide 'was very
nearly responsible for the fall of at least one European government',
we register this as a given fact but feel no conviction of the social
power we see in Kane.

It seems that Welles needs a realistic context in which to place his
supermen. A superman without recognizable human beings under
his control is not a superman but an eccentric. When Susan leaves
Kane, he falls into the position of helpless dependency she had filled
only a moment earlier, and the contrast is shattering. But when
Arkadin falls from Raina's existence, we can only mirror her expression of futile regret. The price he pays for his self-dramatization is
only that of losing an audience. We may feel that we have witnessed
an extraordinary gesture, but it is a sentimental gesture. Arkadin
destroys himself to prove that he has no reason to live. Welles's
other heroes have a reason to take others with them as they die, but
Arkadin is merely an exhibitionist.

10: Touch of Evil

In 1957, through a misunderstanding, Welles returned to Hollywood directing after an absence of almost ten years. The ironies surrounding the genesis of *Touch of Evil* are as dark and bizarre as the film itself. Charlton Heston agreed to appear in a Universal police melodrama, thinking that Welles had been signed to direct it, when actually he had only been signed as an actor. The studio, undaunted by Welles's pariah status in Hollywood, *then* asked him to direct, perhaps figuring that he couldn't go too far out of bounds with the material he was given. He accepted with alacrity, and received no salary as writer or director. He never read the source novel, Whit Masterson's *Badge of Evil*, but found the studio's scenario 'ridiculous', and demanded the right to write his own. He shot the film in the hellish city of Venice, California, later the location for Roger Corman's *The Wild Angels*, and peopled it with a cast which, as Pauline Kael remarks, is 'assembled as perversely as in a nightmare': Marlene Dietrich as a madam, Dennis Weaver as a sex-mad motel clerk (*Psycho* has more in common with *Touch of Evil* than with Robert Bloch's novel), Zsa Zsa Gabor as the owner of a strip joint, Joseph Cotten as a detective, Akim Tamiroff as a small-time hoodlum, Mercedes McCambridge as the leader of a leather-jacket gang. Plus Heston as straight man, Janet Leigh as Heston's naïve, frustrated wife, and Welles himself as heavy.

Nonplussed by the result, the studio called it *Touch of Evil* ('what a silly title', Welles remarked; his title has not been recorded) and slipped it into release without a trade showing. André Bazin congratulated Welles for making a film capable of pleasing both drive-in

Welles in *Touch of Evil*

audiences and serious *cinéastes*, but outside of France it pleased neither. The American audience could afford to ignore Welles. In France, however, where they notice such things, *Touch of Evil* was declared to be a masterpiece. It is richer, more personal and (a vital point) more entertaining than *The Trial*, which is a less deeply felt, more studiedly allegorical treatment of much the same theme. And next to *Chimes at Midnight*, it is his most mature, complex work.

Welles returns to the theme of the law, which he had treated in parodistic form in *The Lady from Shanghai*. There, as in *The Trial*, he concentrates on a seemingly innocent man trapped by an inhuman legal system whose complexities at first seem merely irrational and finally are seen to be the logical extension of the contradictions of character. In *Touch of Evil*, Welles creates a character, the police captain Hank Quinlan, who deftly uses official power for personal and corrupt purposes, like Kane and his newspapers and Arkadin and his financial empire. The emphasis shifts from the 'innocent' who outwits the law to the man who is destroyed by his over-reaching, like Bannister. In *The Trial*, the emphasis again returns to the 'innocent', but the humour of the work is so dark, so abstracted, that we find it too hard to maintain the sympathy which would allow us to see ourselves in Joseph K. Welles denies us the conventional sympathy which his pathetic situation might offer by making Anthony Perkins's K. smug, self-righteous and cruel, and we are turned back on our intellectual understanding of his position. Quinlan is a much more accessible character. His emotions are closer to the surface, though Welles never indulges in sentimentality. Where he differs from K. is that we easily ratify the validity of his emotions, though we condemn his actions; with K., we must transfer our concerns to an abstracted concept of personal responsibility. If repeated viewings of *The Trial* tend to diminish our pleasure in it (it is a film I admire, but don't particularly enjoy), *Touch of Evil* gains in fascination, each viewing revealing new levels of irony, moral complexity and wit. Quinlan is the most likeable Welles hero until Falstaff, but his actions are the most odious of any Welles hero. The enormity of the gulf between his intentions and his actions helps Welles to make one of his most lucid philosophical presentations.

Quinlan's wife was long ago murdered by a man who got off free because Quinlan, then a rookie cop, could not prove the case.

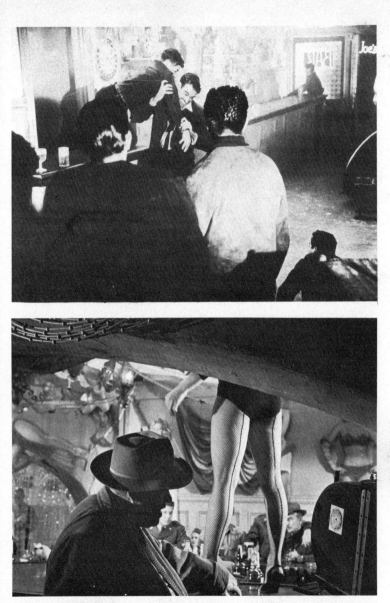

Touch of Evil: (above) Vargas (Charlton Heston) tackles the hoodlums; *(below)* Welles on set

Though 'in some mud hole in Belgium, in 1917, the good Lord done the job for me,' Quinlan has become obsessed by this palpable demonstration of the inadequacy of the law. If a murderer can escape because of lack of evidence, he reasons, why not plant evidence to be sure of capturing the right man? Quinlan's idea is a perfect illustration of Raskolnikov's dictum in *Crime and Punishment*: 'The "extraordinary" man has the right ... in himself ... to permit his conscience to overstep certain obstacles, but only in the event that his ideas (which may sometimes be salutary for all mankind) require it for their fulfilment. If it is necessary for one of these extraordinary people for the fulfilment of his ideas to march over corpses, or wade through blood, then in my opinion, he may in all conscience authorize himself to wade through blood – in proportion, however, to his idea and the degree of its importance – mark that.'

His badge allows Quinlan to make corpses of the men he arrests, and we have his testimony and that of his deputy Menzies that he has never framed anyone who wasn't guilty. Until the chance arrival of an outsider – a Mexican narcotics agent named Vargas (Heston) – Quinlan's methods have never upset anybody. He is an honourable man. But Vargas discovers that Quinlan has planted evidence implicating a Mexican shoe clerk in the murder of a local bigwig, and is appalled. We too are appalled, because we see only the false evidence and have no reason to consider the man guilty. We share Vargas's liberal sympathy for an apparently innocent man, and we condemn Quinlan's actions without reserve. In the last moments of the film we learn that the shoe clerk has confessed: Quinlan was 'right' after all. But the moral issue has already been resolved. The denouement clarifies the difference between law and lynch-law. As the witnesses of his death put it, Quinlan was a great detective, but a lousy cop.

A conventional moralist would have loaded the issue by making the clerk innocent, but Welles forces us to maintain an ironic position. Quinlan's *game leg* tells him that the man is guilty! How outrageous, we agree with Vargas – but if we feel that the man's guilt reverses Quinlan's we have missed the point entirely. In the extraordinary interrogation scenes, a series of long uninterrupted takes in a single apartment (one of which lasts almost five minutes and involves more than sixty camera movements), Welles deviously involves us in Quinlan's machinations. The Mexican is silly, smug, absurd ('the very best shoe clerk the store ever had,' he tells us). Quinlan is brutal, unreasoning, and easily able to demolish the defendant. The Mexican is obviously being persecuted, Quinlan is an obvious bully. But the Mexican offends us by being a fool, and Quinlan makes us admire his godlike insouciance. It is typical of Welles that the people who are right are the people we don't like, and the people who are wrong are admirable. He is a rhetorician who forces us to acknowledge that issues exist apart from their proponents. Or, more precisely, he separates an issue from its proponent in order to free us from sentimental identification, to let us see the issue itself more clearly. If we are to agree with the Mexican that he is being persecuted, we must do this not through facile sympathy with a noble figure of defiance; we must sympathize with a clown. And if we are to condemn Quinlan's actions, we must condemn the actions of a man we see to be adept and, indeed, admirable. The parable about the scorpion and the drowning frog becomes clear. The logic is in principle, not in character.

Welles sets Quinlan off with a beautiful array of counterposing characters. Quinlan's mad passion is understood only by his deputy, Pete Menzies (movingly played by Joseph Calleia). Menzies hears Quinlan's confession in the bar, a confession of motives he has heard many times before. He accepts it while still continuing to prod Quinlan about his methods. Like Leland in *Citizen Kane*, he is committed to love and friendship at the cost of his own integrity. Calleia's mournful tremulousness is a powerful counterpoint to his accumulating moral force. When Quinlan commits murder in a demented attempt to frame Vargas's wife, Menzies realizes that he must make Quinlan admit the truth about himself. As with Leland, he becomes the hero's conscience. 'Quinlan is the god of Menzies,' Welles has commented. 'And, because Menzies worships him, the real theme of the scenario is treason, the terrible impulsion that Menzies has to betray his friend.' Menzies has debased himself by playing Quinlan's accomplice – he has surrendered – and when Quinlan's quest for 'justice' finally drives him to the very act which had provoked the quest, Menzies realizes with terrible clarity the insanity of his own actions. Welles crystallizes all the tensions of the relationship in a powerful 'syllogism' of images: Quinlan long ago saved Menzies's life by stopping a bullet meant for him, causing his game leg and necessitating his use of a cane (this is explained in a scene cut from the film, but remains an implication); Quinlan tacitly admits his guilt by leaving the cane next to the murdered man's body, convincing Menzies to confront him; and, finally, when Quinlan has shot Menzies, only to be himself shot by Menzies, he says, 'That's the second bullet I've stopped for you, partner.' The survivors sum it up as they look at Quinlan's body:

Schwartz: You really liked him, didn't you?
Tanya: The cop did. The one who killed him. He loved him.

Vargas is the holder of the correct ideas; he speaks up for the right principles; he is played by a man who embodies stoic incorruptibility and sincerity. But his posture is stiff, humourless and self-righteous. When he stands up to Quinlan, we know that we are in the presence of a prig. He is colourless next to Quinlan. We admire his tenacity in ferreting out proof of Quinlan's treachery, but we like Quinlan for his candour: 'An old lady on Main Street picked up a shoe. The shoe had a foot in it. We're going to make you pay for that, boy.' If we are going to side with Vargas, we do so fully aware that he has no comprehension of the moral beauty which underlies Quinlan's warped behaviour.

Welles makes a subtle implication in the magnificent opening shot, an unbroken travelling movement which combines the planting of a bomb in a car and its journey through border customs with the passage of Vargas and his wife behind it. If Welles had not filmed the dual journeys in one continuous shot, he would have lost the tension of inevitability, the feeling that what the couple is doing (crossing a border, a metaphor to be re-echoed throughout the film) is inextricable from what is happening to the car. If Welles had cut back and forth from the couple to the car, he would have implied either a parallelism or a contrast. Instead he suspends any kind of moral statement until the couple kiss – and he cuts to the car exploding. An image for the violent disruption of their relationship, clearly, but, even more strongly, a linkage of actions which implies a cause-and-effect relationship. In some unknown way, Welles is saying, something about this couple contains the seeds of violence and murder.

Strangely, the most dangerously ambiguous character in the film, the one of whom we feel the least confident, the one whose motives we least understand and whose purpose we feel to be the most pliable, is Schwartz, the assistant district attorney, who (as played by Mort Mills, later the menacing policeman of *Psycho*, in impeccable suit and tie) appears the most normal, least corrupt of the whole bunch. His complacent acceptance of Quinlan disturbs us, but it is not until he asks off-handedly, 'Who do you like as the killer?' that his moral blindness becomes fully apparent. We feel unsure of Vargas, despite his moral authority, because of his stiff, moronic treatment of his wife, who is ingenuously, absurdly dependent on him. He interrupts their honeymoon to handle the case (a honeymoon in Los Robles!) and packs her off to a motel in the middle of nowhere which proves to be run by the Grande family, the scurviest group of misfits this side of *Los Olvidados*. Whatever respect we have for Vargas as a spokesman for a higher order of justice is steadily undermined by his disregard for his wife's safety. Only after she is drugged, (almost) gang-raped and tied to a bed with a corpse hanging over her head does he realize that he has been derelict in his responsibilities to her. The debasement of the marriage parallels the assaults made on Vargas's complacent assumption that the law is above human meddling. The order that Vargas believes in and represents is artificial, bloodless. After his wife is kidnapped, he abruptly redefines himself: 'I'm no cop now, I'm a husband.' For him, character is logical.

Welles evokes Quinlan's idealistic beginnings in an encounter with Tanya (Dietrich), who knew him in his better days but now fails to recognize him for his paunch and general decrepitude. The brittle evanescence of Sternberg hovers over the scene in which Quinlan wanders from the murder into the brothel on hearing Tanya's playerless pianola. Tanya is totally, unabashedly corrupt. She does not even care to romanticize her function. When the dazed Quinlan asks her if she has been reading the cards, she puffs on her cigar and says that she has been doing the accounts. Still, she is able to tell him, when he demands his fortune, 'Your future is all used up.' The brothel scenes have a soft chiaroscuro about them that is in total contrast to the wild, monstrous shadows and violent camera movements of the rest of the film; Tanya's brothel is a place of rest, of comedy, of dreams. Even Quinlan seems to realize that her solace is professional and disinterested. 'You're a mess, honey,' she tells him. 'You'd better lay off those candy bars.' He grunts, admitting, 'Well, it's either the candy or the hooch. I must say I sure wish it

Touch of Evil: 'You're a mess, honey.' Welles and Dietrich

was your chili I was getting fat on.' She is unimpressed. 'You better watch out. It may be too hot for you.'

For all her cynicism, we can see in Tanya the spirit of Mrs Kane, the evocation of an existence simple in its compassion and unencumbered by any contact with the harshness of reality. But, like Mrs Kane, Tanya cannot offer the hero the consolation of permanence (and it is significant that the heroes' female companions in *Touch of Evil, The Trial, Chimes at Midnight* and *The Immortal Story* are all prostitutes). She will not give him a spurious fortune. Mrs Kane sent Charles to his fortune because she wanted him away from his father. Her choice was between one kind of damnation and another, more honourable kind, and she decided to let him damn himself rather than smother him in illusory security (a lesson Isabel Amberson learned only at the cost of her own life). By now, however, the woman from the past has no compunction in releasing the hero to his fate. Unlike Mrs Kane, she does not suffer; she merely observes and understands. Tanya arrives just as Quinlan falls to his death, betrayed by his passions and killed by his only friend. Her comment is laconic: 'He was some kind of a man. What does it matter what you say about people...' Neither sympathy nor condemnation is called for at the scene of Quinlan's death. He had summed up his contradictions in his actions.

Welles examines the price of illegitimate power, however pure its motive. Vargas tells Quinlan with great conviction, a conviction we share, 'A policeman's job is only easy in a police state. That's the whole *point*, captain. Who's the boss, the cop or the law?' But for Quinlan an abstraction like 'police state' is of no importance. He has chosen to disregard the consequences of following his nature, and accepts the result without complaint. The hideous darkness and orgiastic rhythm of *Touch of Evil* describes perfectly the destruction Quinlan has wrought on the world around him. The Welles hero has progressed far beyond Kane and Arkadin in self-realization. Kane clung to the glass ball, the image of his past; Arkadin vainly invoked the name of his daughter. Quinlan dies in a world so foul that his malignity seems, because of its unsparing candour, to be a virtue.

11: The Trial

'I couldn't put my name to a work that implies man's ultimate surrender. Being on the side of man, I had to show him in his final hour undefeated.'

Welles

Of all Welles's films to date, *The Trial* remains the most difficult to evaluate. I have noted that the unrelieved grimness of its moral tone and the heaviness of its humour make us hesitate to consider it an unqualified success. It begins to exhaust even a sympathetic audience long before the end; perhaps Welles was correct when he said once that a good film could be made from Kafka's novel but that he was not the man to do it. Still, anyone sympathetic to Welles feels reluctant to attack the film, in view of the vituperative comments made by American and British reviewers, including even some of Welles's professed admirers. *The Trial* is clearly all of a piece. Welles has effectively adapted Kafka's narrative to the demands of his own moral universe. The question, for any serious critic, is not whether Welles has 'faithfully' adapted the book (such an argument is aesthetically irresponsible), but to what degree Welles's profoundly personal style can afford to accommodate the characters and meanings of a man almost totally dissimilar in style and temperament.

The problem does not arise in discussing Welles's adaptation of Booth Tarkington's *The Magnificent Ambersons* or Isak Dinesen's *The Immortal Story*. Here we feel no irreconcilable tension between material and realization but only a beneficent contribution, a broadening of Welles's scope. *Mr Arkadin*, which Welles based on his own novel, might have benefited from the detachment demanded by one author's adaptation of another. Some proponents of the *auteur* theory have, however, placed an unfortunate emphasis on the importance of 'tension' in directorial style. The argument that the

141

The Trial: K. (Anthony Perkins) and executioners

significance of a work arises from the tension between the given material and the director's attitude towards it – e.g., Otto Preminger's liberal treatment of conservative material in *Advise and Consent* or John Ford's conservative treatment of liberal material in *Cheyenne Autumn* – would imply, if carried to its extreme, that the richest work would result from a total disparity between material and style, something like Ford directing *A Hard Day's Night*. Few theorists, obviously, would carry the argument that far, but the point is that it is dangerous to treat such tension as an end in itself, rather than as a factor contributing to the totality of the work. Left to himself, Welles would probably not have supplied the intricate journalistic satire of *Kane* or the ambivalence towards social progress of *The Ambersons*, but his world-view shows no strain in accommodating such attitudes. The problem when considering an author's sources is not so much to point out what the author has rejected – a peripheral concern in the case of a successful work – but what he has accepted and has thus made his own.

Kafka's work is essentially comic. His heroes are driven from tranquillity by an inexplicably malevolent force which has fallen upon them totally at random; it is a vicious parody of the doctrine of original sin. There is punishment and guilt but no corresponding cause. The 'sin' is assumed as a prior condition of existence. Kafka's heroes are faceless; they have no power, no stature (but for some ironic bureaucratic authority), and ultimately no dignity. They are not tragic but comic and pathetic. K. realizes at the end of *The Trial* that he is dying 'like a dog'. What is tragic in Kafka is existence in general, the kind of inexorable logic that begins in the commonest actions and proceeds through an endless maze of controvertions of the ordinary, ending in the inevitable death of the hero. K. submits to the knife, unable even to kill himself, which would imply an acknowledgement of responsibility. 'The responsibility for this last failure of his,' the narrator comments, 'lay with him who had not left him the remnant of strength necessary for the deed.' We are told that Kafka would laugh to himself while reading parts of *The Trial* to his friends. If this strikes us as curious, we should consider that the godlike narrator of *The Trial* is his own tragedian. The desolation of Kafka's world is the result of a prior act of will on the part of its creator, who is not God, certainly, but Kafka. The powerless beings under his control are acting out the drama of his own over-

142

The Trial: Anthony Perkins

weening pride. It is Kafka who has not left K. the remnant of
strength necessary to act of his own volition. It is Kafka who denies
meaning to his characters' lives and refuses to consider the possibility of a higher order. Pity his characters – for their impotence,
which they are tempted to regard with guilt, is but a comic statement of their creator's preordination of defeat as the universal
principle.

This is, of course, the exact inverse of Welles's position. As
creator he holds his heroes to a code of justice and condemns their
violation of its principles, not their ignorance of principle. He forces
his heroes to choose between responsible self-determination and
godlike arrogance. 'All the characters I've played are various forms
of Faust,' he has stated. 'I hate all forms of Faust, because I believe
it's impossible for man to be great without admitting there is
something greater than himself – either the law or God or art – but
there must be something greater than man. I have sympathy for
those characters – humanly but not morally.' Given this seemingly
irreconcilable conflict between Kafka's material and Welles's philosophical attitude, we can expect an extreme dialectical tension
between the characters' actions and the author's view of them. If we
must continue to talk of Welles and Kafka – as we do not need to

talk of Welles and Tarkington, but may refer only to Welles – it is because the story proceeds not so much by emotional intensification as through rhetorical interplay. What Welles has done in taking *The Trial* as his basis is to treat the Kafka theme of preordained defeat as a constant challenge to the stability of his own moral order.

And Welles's egocentric visual style is at a pole from Kafka's method of presentation. Of all film-makers, Alfred Hitchcock is the closest to Kafka. His style has the same lucidity and syntactical logic, the same orderliness and simplicity mocking the chaos of the world situation, though with an accompanying tragic sense perhaps attributable to his sceptical Catholicism. *The Wrong Man*, the admirable 'rough draft' for *North by Northwest* drawn from an actual incident of an arrest similar to that in *The Trial*, lacks the giddy humour of Hitchcock's later film but could well serve as a step-by-step illustration of how to film the nightmarish aspect of Kafka's world. Kafka's method is to describe each of his settings in terms of naturalistic time and space, and then to introduce an illogical system of character relationships which makes the seeming logic of time and space a parody of a stable world order. Welles completely distorts time and space here, juxtaposing patently disparate locales and cutting on K.'s movement out of and into each of these otherwise unrelated settings, thus making the universe totally a function of K.'s actions. The denouement conveys a spatial idea that Welles had planned to express in more schematic fashion before he was given a gigantic abandoned railway station as his only set. 'The production, as I had sketched it,' he explains, 'comprised sets that gradually disappear. The number of realistic elements were to become fewer and fewer and the public would become aware of it, to the point where the scene would be reduced to free space, as if everything had dissolved.' In the final images, the baroque shapes of *The Trial's* space-time continuum are abstracted into a thin line between bare earth and grey sky, and the struggle of Joseph K. does indeed become the centre of the universe.

To understand the full complexity of Welles's point of view here, we must assess the exact nature of his rhetoric. A crucial point is his dual presence both as author and in the person of the Advocate. The character assumes a more important function than in the novel, in which he serves mainly to distract K. farther and farther from the possibility of effectively resolving his case. Welles's demonic playing

The Trial: K. and the law (Anthony Perkins)

makes the Advocate not a distraction but the very embodiment of the temptation against which K. must struggle. This is confirmed by the Advocate's reappearance in the cathedral at the end, taking over the interrogatory function Kafka assigned to a priest. In the monstrous immobility – one can almost say lack of spiritual identity – to which the Advocate has given himself over, and in the totally subservient position of his client Block (who acts 'like a dog'), K. can see clearly the implications of despair. Like Kurtz in *Heart of Darkness*, Welles's Advocate presents the hero with a vision of chaos which makes possible the hero's moral victory.

Few other films have been offered in rhetorical exchange with another work; among the examples are *Rio Bravo* to *High Noon* and *Le Mépris* to *The Odyssey*. Welles does not assume that his audience has *read* Kafka's novel; such an assumption would place the work in the realm of criticism rather than of artistic expression, and Welles is no polemicist. Instead, he is careful to keep us constantly aware of a philosophical position inimical to his own. We can see this most clearly in the cathedral scene, which has the Advocate reciting Kafka's parable of the law – the tale of a man who waits his entire life before a great door, which is closed without a word from behind it – and K., making a climactic assertion of personal responsibility, interrupting him to speak for Welles's position. The ensuing interchange, written almost entirely by Welles, crystallizes the conflict in K.'s mind and precipitates his immediate destruction. In the light of the focal point it occupies in the drama, it deserves quoting in full:

Advocate: Some commentators have pointed out that the man came to the door of his own free will.

K.: And we're supposed to swallow all that? It's all true?

Advocate: You needn't accept everything as true – only what's necessary.

K.: God, what a miserable conclusion. It turns lying into a universal principle.

Advocate: Attempting to defy the court by such an obviously mad gesture – you hope to plead insanity? You've laid some foundation for that claim by appearing to believe yourself the victim of some kind of conspiracy.

K.: That's a symptom of lunacy, isn't it?

Advocate: Delusions of persecution . . .

K.: Delusions?

Advocate: Well?

K.: I don't pretend to be a martyr, no.

Advocate: Not even . . . a victim of society?

K.: I am a member of society.

Advocate: You think you can persuade the court that you're not responsible by reason of lunacy?

K.: I think that's what the court wants me to believe. Yes, that's the conspiracy – persuade us all that the whole world is crazy – formless, meaningless, absurd! That's the dirty game. So I've lost my case. What of it? You – you're losing too. It's all lost. Lost – so what? Does that sentence the entire universe to lunacy?

Enter a priest.

Priest: Can't you see anything at all?

K.: Of course. I'm responsible.

Priest: My son —

K.: I am not your son.

The subtle difference between K.'s position and Welles's is that Welles endorses K.'s principle – an individual has the power to prove the existence of an order greater than himself – but does not endorse K.'s subsequent action of arrogant destructiveness. Society for Welles is a projection of the hero's conscience; in a profound image he has K.'s executioners make their final appearance by emerging from behind his body on the steps of the cathedral. But

Welles's K. lets nothing outlive him. In an ecstatic solipsistic gesture he hurls the executioners' dynamite away from him into an empty landscape. It explodes in a permutation of blasts culminating in the frozen image of a mushroom cloud, which is followed only by a godlike light streaming from a projector as the author identifies himself from the fourth dimension. K.'s tragic decision to be the agent of universal destruction is the ratification of his final dignity, but it is also the measure of his moral stature. The desolation of the final landscape of *The Trial* is even more vast than that of *Touch of Evil*. In the very act of proving that there is an order to the universe, K. presumes to judge the universe. It is well that he realizes his responsibility for his individual actions, but when he extends his responsibility to the universe in general, he oversteps the boundary between man and superman.

K.'s act of defiance redeems the formlessness around him by asserting man's position as master of his destiny, but it creates a new, more deadly chaos – the uncontrolled power of the ego. Kafka reassures us by postulating a sympathetic, good-willed, amorphous hero. If he is defeated, we are at least given the option of considering him an innocent victim. He can be considered guilty only if we consider him an active agent of the destructive system, and Kafka conveys this only in the comic sense of a rat intuitively knowing his way to the end of the maze. In Welles's terms, K. is guilty first of all because he has allowed himself to function as part of a system destructive of free will. We understand this through Anthony Perkins's skilful playing of K. as a self-righteous bureaucrat foolishly revelling in his status as assistant manager of his department, with attendant power to punish subordinates. The final irony, though, is that K., in Welles's words, 'is not guilty as accused, but he is guilty all the same'. His guilt, in the final analysis, is the sin of pride. It is significant of Welles's darkening attitude that the hitherto helpless K., on realizing his moral power, should immediately use it to a more evil effect than even Macbeth or Arkadin could manage. Macbeth's actions resulted in the fall of a dynasty, Arkadin's nearly resulted in the fall of several European governments; but the petty, self-pitying, naïve, childish K. has it in him to destroy the universe.

12: Chimes at Midnight

Chimes at Midnight is Welles's masterpiece, the fullest, most completely realized expression of everything he had been working towards since *Citizen Kane*, which itself was more an end than a beginning. The younger Welles was obsessed with the problem of construction, and solved it perfectly with a style which locked the apparently powerful hero into an ironic vice of which he was almost totally unaware. We could not be farther from the characters, and perhaps this distancing, however suited to the telling of a story of futile omnipotence, was an acknowledgement of artistic immaturity on Welles's part: faced with the problem of defining himself, he contrived a style to prove that definition is illusory. In *Chimes at Midnight*, Welles has fused his own viewpoint and that of his hero into a direct communication of emotion. His style, though it is every bit as deliberate and controlled as in *Kane*, no longer demands our attention for itself. There is nothing here to correspond with *Kane's* mirror trickery; there *is* a battle sequence which is one of the greatest achievements in action direction in the history of the cinema, and which moreover is constructed in a highly rhetorical pattern, almost as tightly as a fugue, but it presents itself to the audience not as an artistic demonstration but as an overwhelming physical experience.

I think that here Welles finds himself where Beethoven found himself when he replaced musical instruments with voices in the Ninth Symphony: he has broken the bounds of his tools (the camera and the cutting bench) and has given everything over to human instruments (his actors). When told that no one could possibly sing some of the notes he had written, Beethoven replied that it was no concern of his. Welles is more pragmatic – since he himself must make the actors correspond to his purposes – but there is the same rhapsodic exhilaration in his submersion into faces and voices. As Pierre Duboeuf has put it, 'He broods with a disquiet like Rembrandt's over his own face, and it is not inconsequential that he finds there other attunements, accents less brilliant but more human, which he substitutes for the dazzling flashes of the past.' We feel, as we do in *The Magnificent Ambersons*, that Welles is rejecting the mask of self-conscious stylization in order to find himself in a relaxed, sensual spontaneity. A crucial difference, however, is that Welles hid himself behind the camera in *The Ambersons*, revealing himself through his attitude towards other people, and here he looms before us buoyantly fat, literally and figuratively much more himself than he has ever been before.

And, appropriately, the story he is telling is the story of a man who is completely candid, a man whose complete lack of pretence, when confronted with the world's demands of responsibility and self-denial, becomes the very cause of his destruction. During production, Welles explained his intentions: '*Chimes* should be very plain on the visual level because above all it is a very real human story ... The Falstaff story is the best in Shakespeare – not the best play, but the best story . . . Everything of importance in the film should be found on the faces; on these faces that whole universe I was speaking of should be found. I imagine that it will be the film of my life in terms of close-ups ... A story like *Chimes* demands them, because the moment we step back and separate ourselves from the faces, we see the people in period costumes and many actors in the foreground. The closer we are to the face, the more universal it becomes. *Chimes* is a sombre comedy, the story of the betrayal of friendship.' And after the film was completed, he observed, '*The Ambersons* and *Chimes at Midnight* represent more than anything else what I would like to do in films ... what I am trying to discover now in films is not technical surprises or shocks, but a more complete unity of forms, of shapes. That's what I'm reaching for, what I hope is true. If it is, then I'm reaching maturity as an artist. If it isn't true, then I'm in decadence, you know?'

The reader of these descriptions should not suppose that *Chimes* is as fluid and deceptively nonchalant as a Renoir film; far from it.

When we talk about a 'plain' style, we mean that the camera is at the service of the actors, and not vice versa (as in *The Trial*, for instance). When a director matures, his work becomes more lucid, more direct, allowing room for deeper audience response; as Truffaut has put it, what is in front of the camera becomes more important. And 'direct', in the complex rhetorical world of Welles's films, means not that the issues are simplified, but that their presentation is – we feel them with more intensity and passion. Compare the climax of *Kane*, in which Kane slaps Susan, to the muted climax of *Chimes at Midnight*, in which Hal banishes Falstaff and the old man murmurs, 'Master Shallow, I owe you a thousand pound.' The scene in *Kane* is exciting and moving, but its theatricality tends to widen the gulf between Kane's emotions and our comprehension of them. If *Citizen Kane* has a flaw, it is in its relative dispassion – a scheme in which we are so far removed from the hero that we may easily watch his struggle with mere fascination. *Kane* is perhaps too mathematical in conception; the true hero, it is not unfitting to say, is not Kane but Welles himself. But in *Chimes* there is finally no distance between Welles and Falstaff; a simple exchange of close-ups between Hal and Falstaff conveys emotions infinitely deeper than does Kane's explosive action. It is the difference between the expression of an emotion and the sharing of an emotion.

Welles's liberties with the text generally escape our notice, extreme as they are, not only because he has so smoothly transformed Shakespeare's concerns into his own but because his concentration on Falstaff enables him to achieve a dramatic focus which Shakespeare's historical concerns tend at times to dilute. The story is taken from *1 Henry IV* and *2 Henry IV*, with bits from *Henry V*, *The Merry Wives of Windsor* and *Richard II*, and a narration from Holinshed's *Chronicles*. Shakespeare seems to have intended Falstaff as a relatively simple comic counterpoint to the King-Prince-Hotspur story in the first part of *Henry IV* (as the rather awkward alternation of historical and comic scenes would suggest) and only gradually discovered that Falstaff was so profound a character that he all but overshadowed the drama of kingship. Not only the greater length given to Falstaff's scenes but the immeasurably more fluid structure of the second part – in which the imbalance threatened by Falstaff's pre-eminence becomes qualified by the crisis in his relationship with the Prince – attest to Shakespeare's fully ripened

Chimes at Midnight: 'a sombre comedy.' Welles as Falstaff

understanding of Falstaff's meaning. We have of course been prepared for the rejection of Falstaff by the great tavern scene in the first part, but in the second, Falstaff takes on a graver aspect, not only in Hal's eyes as a threat to his princely dignity but in his own as well. Images of age, disease and death suddenly proliferate, and the gay denunciations of honour give way to sober, more closely reasoned (and more witty) inward reflection. Shakespeare also creates four new companions for Falstaff – Pistol, Doll Tearsheet, Shallow, and Silence – as if to compensate for Hal's growing absorption into himself. 'In the first part of the play,' Welles comments, 'the Hotspur subplot keeps the business of the triangle between the King, his son and Falstaff (who is a sort of foster father) from dominating. But in my film, which is made to tell, essentially, the story of that triangle, there are bound to be values which can't exist as it is played in the original. It's really quite a different drama.'

We can see in Welles's decision to make Hal a subordinate figure to Falstaff not only an extremely ironic attitude towards the idea of the 'Christian king' (a concept as alien to Welles as it is central to

Chimes at Midnight: Falstaff in the tavern (Welles, Margaret Rutherford, Jeanne Moreau)

Shakespeare and, in a modern guise, to John Ford, from whom Welles borrows greatly in this film) but also a more definite emphasis on the essential *goodness* of Falstaff's character, the tragic nobility of even those attributes – his disregard of health and social discretion – which will inevitably destroy him. The act of banishment by Shakespeare's Hal is not a tragic decision; it is the seal of moral maturity, the 'noble change' he proclaims to the 'incredulous world'. The war he will wage on France as Henry V, which Shakespeare is at pains to present in that play as the God-given and ancestrally determined right of empire, becomes in *Chimes at Midnight* a totally unmotivated, madly wilful action. On our first sight of Hal after the ceremony of coronation, he proclaims the war with no reason given but for a sentry's cry of 'No king of England, if not king of France!' In other words, Hal, on accepting responsibility, immediately puts it to blindly destructive ends, just as K. did in *The Trial*. Welles does not invoke, as Shakespeare does, a higher imperative for Hal's action, presenting it solely as a function of his will. Welles's Hal is as truly a tragic figure as is his father, who had wrested his kingdom illegitimately from Richard and was then doomed to face unceasing rebellion.

Hal comes into his crown legitimately, by right of birth, and in Shakespeare's terms is thus rightfully able to purpose the building of

Chimes at Midnight: Hal and Falstaff (Keith Baxter, Welles)

an empire. But for Welles (for Shakespeare too, but to a lesser degree of emphasis), Hal has lost the better part of himself in his rejection of Falstaff and all he stands for. The banishment is inevitable if he is to acquiesce to his position of power, but the price of the world dominion he will thus achieve is the subjection of his own moral nature, as Welles makes clear in the arbitrariness of his first action after the banishment. Hal's final words to Falstaff have a meaning entirely opposite to their meaning in the play: 'Being awaked, I do despise my dream ... Presume not that I am the thing I was ... I have turned away my former self.' And his last words in the film show how much he has deluded himself: 'We consider it was excess of wine that set him on.' Welles holds on the new king's pose of bemused reflection for several long seconds, and in the next shot shows us Poins eating an apple (the end of innocence) and Falstaff's coffin.

For Shakespeare, Falstaff is essentially a comic figure because, while completely innocent, he is destructive of kingly power, and must be sacrificed without question to the demands of a greater order. For Welles, the greater order is *Falstaff*, and Hal sacrifices both Falstaff and himself in the submission to his own will. Hal is as destructive of innocence as Falstaff is of kingship. And Welles gives us a strong sense of a curious moral trait of Falstaff's which several

Shakespearean commentators have pointed out: though innocent, he seeks out the very force which will destroy him. In this we can see a quality in Falstaff which precludes calling him a merely comic figure. If we can call *Chimes at Midnight* the tragedy of Falstaff (and we can, even though he makes moral decisions only by instinct), it is tragedy perhaps more in the Aristotelian than in the Shakespearean sense of the term. Welles's description of Falstaff is profound: 'What is difficult about Falstaff, I believe, is that he is the greatest conception of a good man, the most completely good man, in all drama. His faults are so small and he makes tremendous jokes out of little faults. But his goodness is like bread, like wine ... And that was why I lost the comedy. The more I played it, the more I felt that I was playing Shakespeare's good, pure man.'

We do not see in Falstaff an essentially noble man of extraordinary gifts who destroys himself through a grave flaw in his nature which is also the source of his nobility; we see in him something rather more subtle and less absolute – a man of extraordinary gifts which destroy him because he fails to acknowledge their irreconcilable conflict with the nature of the world. His moral blindness (which is to say his childlike candour, an attribute he is sometimes apt to use as a ploy) is his only flaw. Much as Othello was blind to the existence of the kind of power Iago possessed, Falstaff is blind to the possibility that Hal could reject his gift of absolute love. A. C. Bradley remarks of Othello that we share his 'triumphant scorn for the fetters of the flesh and the littleness of all the lives that must survive him.' Falstaff we can say has a triumphant acceptance of the absoluteness of the flesh and a spontaneous respect for all the lives around him.

The likeness of Hal to Iago is more than casual. Just as his father has been careful to cover the illegitimacy of his kingship with actions which assert his legitimacy – the vanquishing of internal rebellion – Hal schools himself in hypocrisy. From the first, Welles makes clear that Hal's merry-making with Falstaff is fraudulent, both a distraction from his impending moral crisis and a testing of his ability to withstand the temptations of instinct. Iago's 'I am not what I am' finds many echoes in Hal, from his first soliloquy ('... herein will I imitate the sun, / Who doth permit the base contagious clouds / To smother up his beauty from the world'), delivered with Falstaff musing vaguely in the background, to his final 'Presume not that I am the thing I was,' which leaves Falstaff destitute and uncomprehending. A great deal of the film's pathos and irony comes from the reversal of old and young men's roles. Falstaff's innocence is a sublimely defiant gesture on Welles's part. As a young man he played both Falstaff and Richard III in *Five Kings*, as if to impart a Jekyll-and-Hyde duplicity to the character. Now, as an old man, he makes Falstaff's constant protestations of youth an accusation not only of Hal's unnatural suppression of youth but of death itself. Much more than in Shakespeare, the spectacle of an old man shepherding the revels of a saturnine young man strikes us as a bitter defiance of age and the logic of destiny. Falstaff seeks out Hal because Hal is the least capable, due to his princehood, of casting off responsibilities and the promise of power, and when this ultimate test of his goodness fails, Falstaff fails with it. The heroism lies in the disparity between the greatness of the purpose and the inadequacy of the means.

When a tragic hero is destroyed, Bradley remarks, the primary impression is of *waste*. Waste is our feeling when Welles, at the end, shows Falstaff's huge coffin being wheeled slowly across a barren landscape with only a quiescent castle breaking the line of the horizon, the narrator telling us of Hal, 'a majesty was he that both lived and died a pattern in princehood, a lodestar in honour, and famous to the world alway.' We know that what the narrator is saying is literally true (it was written of the historical Henry V, who had Sir John Oldcastle, Falstaff's prototype, executed for treason), but we cannot help sense the tragic irony as we see the remnants of Hal's humanity being carted away. His expressions and carriage during the banishment speech convey that mingled grandeur and grief-stricken horror that came so naturally to his father after a lifetime of scheming, and when he turns away from Falstaff into a tableau of banners and shields, he becomes a smaller and smaller figure vanishing into the endlessly repetitive corridors of history. If we never sympathize fully with Hal, if we feel, as Welles does, that there is something 'beady-eyed and self-regarding' about him even after he becomes king, we never cease to admire him, even in his tragic folly.

Thanks to Keith Baxter's marvellous performance – next to John Gielgud's incomparable Henry IV the finest in a near-perfect supporting cast – Hal is dignified and comprehensible even at his

Chimes at Midnight: The battle at Shrewsbury. The beginning . . .

cruellest and most vain. Welles's instincts are acute here, for the unpleasantness of Joseph K. is almost fatal to *The Trial*, and Hal, who quite resembles K. in his self-righteousness, needs a sense of human dignity and compassion to make him a suitable subject of Falstaff's attention and to make him fully aware of what he is rejecting when he banishes Falstaff. Hal fills us with awe in that chilling moment when he turns from Falstaff and whispers to himself, 'At the end, try the man,' as if reciting a prayer; in his sudden childlike humility when his father appears, wraith-like, and demands his crown; and most of all in his powerful, serene silence after the battle, when he drops his pot of ale and walks mutely off to follow his destiny. Welles creates a mythic finality about Hal when, cutting away from Hotspur resolving to duel him to the death, he shows us a cloud of dust, which rises to reveal Hal standing helmet and shield in hand on the battlefield (a copy of Ford's introduction of John Wayne in *Stagecoach*, dust rising to show him with rifle in one arm and saddle in the other).

Death hangs over the entire film, and the gaiety seems desperate.

. . . and the end

Both Hal's foster-father and his real father are dying, and he is too preoccupied with his own legendary future to be of solace to either. His fun takes odd and vicious forms, as if he were reproaching both himself, for wasting time, and the butts of his humour, for encouraging him. He wants to see Falstaff 'sweat to death' running from the Gad's Hill robbery, wants to expose him as a monstrous liar, wants to 'beat him before his whore'. One critic has suggested that in the first part of *Henry IV*, Hal is killing his patricidal tendencies (by killing Hotspur, his father's rival), and in the second part is killing his libido, his narcissistic self-adoration (Falstaff, of course), in order to prepare himself for the assumption of kingship. Welles replaces this sense of 'penance' with a sense of vertiginous self-destruction. Like his father, like Hotspur, like, indeed, Falstaff, Hal has sought precisely the course which will destroy him. Hal is frightening because he is so young and yet seems so old. Welles draws a striking parallel in the feelings of Hal and both his 'fathers' when he follows the king's speech on sleep with Hal telling Poins, 'Before God, I am exceeding weary,' and Falstaff murmuring, 'S'blood, I'm as melancholy as a gibbed cat or a lugged bear.'

Bells ringing in the distance give funereal punctuation to the very first scenes in the film, and motives of rejection and farewell are dominant throughout. The battle sequence, the cataclysm of destruction at the centre of the film, begins in splendid romantic exuberance and ends with agonizingly slow, ponderous clouts from soldiers writhing dully in the mud. Welles edits the battle on the principle of 'a blow given, a blow received', and the predominant feeling is of a monumental impasse, of incredible exertion without effect. Falstaff's flesh finally gets the better of him, and he lies helplessly sprawled in bed as Hal and Poins taunt him before Doll Tearsheet, his wit his only reprieve. The king seems chilled and mummified in his huge tomb-like castle. Hal and Hotspur seem almost inert when they duel in their armour shells. But Falstaff! Falstaff runs with a breathtakingly funny agility through the charging troops (a stroke of genius), and weaves his way through an unheeding, mindless tavern full of dancers. But he does not disappear into the aimless masses; he seems doomed to stand out awkwardly from the landscape, like a castle. Everything in the film is on the verge of slowing to a standstill.

But for the battle sequence, *Chimes at Midnight* has none of the violent movements from exhilaration to dejection of Welles's earlier films; its equipoise reflects an achieved serenity. Throughout the film, most bitterly in the strained play-acting between Hal and Falstaff in the tavern scene which foreshadows the climax, the awareness of destruction is present even in moments of 'respite'. Falstaff battles this awareness throughout; his attempts to ignore it provide the comedy. He has none of Kane's guile and worldly ability, and his greatness presents itself as a monstrous jest impossible to ignore but easy to dismiss. He demands nothing but attention, and offers all of himself in return. His egocentricity, like his body, is carried past the ridiculous into the sublime, to the point of melancholia. He fears nothing but death, and reproaches Doll Tearsheet with, 'Thou'lt forget me when I am gone.' It is unlikely that Welles as director or actor will achieve again so moving a scene as that of Falstaff's expulsion. With the author's consent we may feel superior to Kane, but we are never superior to Falstaff. He is naked before us. *Chimes at Midnight* is Welles's testament.

13: The Immortal Story

A generation ago, in *The Lady from Shanghai*, Welles (in the guise of a young sailor) told us that Macao was the wickedest city in the world. He said it with bravado, hoping to impress the young lady who would later try to destroy him. Welles made sport of a naïve young man's deadly tendency to be siphoned on to the most malign of characters – a descent into the maëlstrom. The powers of evil, the lawyer, his wife, and his partner, set up a drama to ensnare the young sailor. In *The Immortal Story*, Welles uses this fable as the basis of a philosophical inquisition. His source, Isak Dinesen's novella, reads like a *précis* of his themes, and he follows it quite closely, shading in his own rhythms and overtones. His hero, Mr Clay, a moribund and fabulously wealthy Macao merchant, wants to prove his power by making the archetypal sailor's story – the story of a rich old man who hires a young sailor to impregnate his wife – pass from legend into fact. 'I don't like pretence,' he muses. 'I don't like prophecies. I like facts . . . People should only record things which have already happened.'

The Lady from Shanghai is packed with bewildering action; almost nothing happens in *The Immortal Story*. But for a short chorus of merchants in an early scene and the handful of Chinese who pass through as mute witnesses, the only people in the film are the four principals: Clay, his clerk Levinsky, the young sailor, and Virginie, the woman Levinsky hires to play the part of Clay's wife. A courtyard, two sparse rooms, and Clay's mansion form the whole of the setting, and two tattered sails in the foreground of the opening shot suffice to indicate the existence of the outside world. This is an

The Immortal Story: Roger Coggio, Jeanne Moreau

interior drama, a meditation. The old man is disconcerted when he finds that all three of his puppets also know the sailor's story; this is an omen, a definition of the forces he will have to overstep to carry out his will. He continues undaunted, bursting into the bedchamber, unable to conceal his passion: 'Because you move without pain, you think you move at your own will. Not so – you move at my bidding. Two young, strong and lusty jumping-jacks in this old hand of mine!'

Welles is, as he has said, primarily a man of ideas, and each of his films is to some extent a philosophical drama. *The Immortal Story* is the most theatrical work in Welles's career. The stage is simple and bare, the props are laid out for our inspection, the issues are stated and reiterated in different keys, and the characters are aware of their roles. A further peculiarity: *The Immortal Story* is a miniature, scarcely an hour long, and it is Welles's first film in colour since *It's All True.* The colour is soft and dreamlike, recalling Fellini's statement that colour in movies is 'like breathing underwater' because 'cinema is movement; colour is immobility'. *The Immortal Story* is a drama of ideas, linear and intellectually direct. But it is emotionally mysterious, developing a tension between immobility and purpose.

Citizen Kane is about mystery, certainly, but the mystery of *fact*. With its maze-like system of cross-references, it strikes me as essen-

The Immortal Story: Welles as Mr Clay

tially evasive, centrifugal (which is not to judge it, only to explain it). Welles assembles all the facts, disproves all of them, and declares his unwillingness to define the hero. We are made to understand the meaning of legend and to wonder at the meaning of fact. We see, hear and feel much about Kane (much more than about Mr Clay), but we know that we do not understand him. *The Immortal Story* approaches legend from the inside out. It is centripetal – *Kane* in negative. But because the making of legend is itself a subjective process, its meaning determined in the mind of its beholder, *The Immortal Story* seems to me to strike into the heart of the matter. What it loses in breadth it gains in lucidity. It omits all that is peripheral to Clay, and defines him as the doer of an essential deed, which in one stroke ennobles him and renders meaningless his prior existence. This is Welles's *Tempest.* We are taken directly into the mind of the creator, and leave our spectators' seats to witness the pulling of the strings above the stage. Clay's musings coincide with the flow of the author's reasoning; when the mechanics of the story have been set completely in motion, Clay dies and the author withdraws after allowing Levinsky to make a final statement of the theme. The screen dissolves to *white*; darkness would be inappropriate to our lucidity.

In the late work of great directors, the youthful delight in flaunt-

161

ing one's tools and one's splendid flashes of insight gives way to a clear-eyed simplicity which the immature and the insecure can easily mistake for senile fixation. Renoir gives us *Le Caporal Epinglé*, Ford *The Man Who Shot Liberty Valance*, Lubitsch *Heaven Can Wait*, Hawks *El Dorado*, Dreyer *Gertrud*, Welles *The Immortal Story*. If it comes to Clay in his last moments to dare the impossible – if it comes to Welles to eschew camera movements and bizarre perspectives – it is because he has seen everything happen. As Clay eats a solitary dinner, his face reflected in a last, nostalgic, melancholy series of mirrors, Welles tells us, 'It was only natural that things should be as they were, because he had willed them to be so.' And yet there is something Clay has not touched, cannot touch, something his machinations call up and cannot dispel. In the extraordinary erotic scenes which lie at the core of the film, Welles shifts suddenly, breathtakingly, to the rapturous intimacy of a hand-held camera as Virginie drifts naked through the bedchamber blowing out the candles in grave preparation for love-making (recapturing a scene from *The Scarlet Empress*, one of the many echoes of Sternberg in this delicately masochistic film). The young sailor enters to find her lying nude in the bed, her arms crossed over her breasts as if in mingled shame and self-protection, and during his undressing Welles gives us magnificent close-ups of her face, her mouth, her eyes. Despite the frank surrender of Elsa in *The Lady from Shanghai*, there was no nudity, no overt eroticism in that strangely chaste film. But here the tentative, spontaneous attraction between the two is an assertion of defiant tenderness, a mockery of Clay's massive, rotting flesh. No Welles hero, not even Quinlan or Falstaff, is closer to decay than this bitter old man.

In his last two films, Welles has moved ever closer to the faces of his characters. It is a hard-won conclusion. Earlier in his career, he had avoided, almost feared, close-ups, preferring the distancing of rhetoric and the qualification of irony. The faces were masks, and the cool baroque style reflected the desperation of his characters' self-deception. *Mr Arkadin* is the apogee of this tendency; from that point on, his characters have been increasingly willing to admit their duplicity. In *The Immortal Story*, everything happens in the glances passed from one person to another, and in their echoes on the face of the hero. Welles has come full circle from the reporter's futile investigation in *Kane*; the story has worked its way back to its source, the story-teller and his audience. K. found it 'a miserable conclusion' that lying should be regarded as a universal principle; Clay, like Falstaff, devotes himself to turning lying into truth. Why then does he die when his drama is consummated? He doesn't die in the book. The book's sailor entrusts Levinsky with a precious shell as a parting gift to Virginie; Welles has the sailor give it to Clay himself for deliverance to her, and a sudden close-up of the shell rocking back and forth on the floor of the veranda where Clay sits shows us that the old man has died.

Welles is not, like Chaplin, a solipsist, though his heroes are. At their deaths, the world flies apart from its bearings – signified usually by the wrenching of chronology and by the grandiosity of their death scenes – but Welles's style gives an ironic qualification to their solipsism. The unfortunate Othello and Arkadin commit suicide, but no Welles hero offers himself up as a martyr, as Chaplin does in *Monsieur Verdoux*. The Welles hero dies fighting, and if he takes the world with him at the end, the act makes clear the presumption implicit in his defiance. Welles is a tragedian. He squares his accounts with the world.

The Immortal Story differs from previous Welles films in that its prologue – usually his instrument for invoking a prescience of death – concerns itself with *past*, not future, destruction. A chorus of three merchants, lesser Clays (an invention of Welles's), discuss briefly and pointedly the circumstances under which Clay drove his partner (Virginie's father) to suicide and took over his mansion. Welles's earlier heroes looked to the past for the comforting, if illusory, memories of innocence; Clay reveres the past, but only because it confirms his present position. He has Levinsky read his old account books to him, and scorns the prophecy of Isaiah ('. . . in the wilderness shall waters break out') that Levinsky carries with him. Innocence, desire and fecundity have no value for him. He contrasts the sailor's ideals with the solidity of gold: 'He's young. Eh, Levinsky? He's full of the juices of life. He has blood in him. I suppose he's got tears. He longs, yearns for the things which dissolve people – for friendship, for love . . . And gold, my young sailor, is solid, it's hard, it's proof against dissolution.' Clay's realization of the sailor's story is a gesture of contempt towards prophecy, an attempt to turn possibility into the *passé*, but both Levinsky and Virginie prophesy several times that Clay's latest venture will be the

cause of his death. Clay believes that it is the future which is dangerous, because it means death, but it is finally the machinery of the past, the sum of his delusions, which leads him to destruction.

The past tense of the prologue warns us that the story will not so much concern a hero's attempts to recapture the past as his attempts to escape it. But where can he escape? The glass ball at the beginning of *Kane*, like the prologue to *The Ambersons*, summons up feelings of mystery and romance. The merchants' grim analysis in *The Immortal Story* leaves us in desolation, and it is only at the *end* that Welles invokes possibility – in the shell, which gives out the sound of the sea, a message from another world. Thus the typical pattern of a Welles film is exactly reversed, and the dropping of the shell has a meaning quite unlike the dropping of the glass ball. When Kane dies, our feeling is of awe and excitement, and the shattering of the ball is thrilling – we share the grandeur of Kane's release. It is only subsequently that we are made aware of the feelings of loss and futility associated with the ball. By the time that Clay drops the shell, however, we have faced the fact that he has obliterated all the alternatives to the bleakness of self-serving. Then, when we see the noiselessly swaying, mute shell (we do not see it drop), we realize suddenly, with great force and compression, that there has always been an alternative – the liberating voice of mystery unheeded. The sensation of discovery coincides with the moment of destruction.

Clay dies because his ego, his consciousness, has overwhelmed him. Virginie looks quietly away as Levinsky pronounces his master's epitaph: 'It's very hard on people who want things so badly that they can't do without them. If they can't get these things, it's hard. And when they do get them, surely it is very hard.' He puts the shell to his ear and listens to the echo of some long-vanished wave. 'I have heard it before, long ago . . . but where?' The *futility* of Kane's life is epitomised by the burning of the sled at the end of the film; forgotten *possibility* is Clay's final perception. Half a lifetime lies between the meticulous qualification of *Citizen Kane* and the impassioned simplicity of *The Immortal Story*. The inversion of the emphasis reminds us that Welles's deepest concerns are not with failure but with potentiality.

A Catalogue of Orson Welles's Career

I have been aided in the preparation of this catalogue by information in Peter Noble's *The Fabulous Orson Welles*, London, 1956; Andrè Bazin's filmography in *Cahiers du Cinéma*, Paris, June 1958; and Peter Cowie's *The Cinema of Orson Welles*, London and New York, 1965. Much of the information printed here is newly collected.

George Orson Welles was born in Kenosha, Wisconsin, on 6 May 1915 to Richard Head Welles, an inventor, and Beatrice Ives Welles, a concert pianist. He had an older brother, Richard, who became a forester. Orson spent much of his youth in Chicago, which he considers his home town. When his mother died in 1923, he began travelling around the world with his father, spending a good deal of time in China. He entered Washington Grade School in Madison, Wisconsin, in 1925, but left after one term. In 1926, he entered Roger Hill's Todd School in Woodstock, Illinois, where he became active in theatre. His father died the following year, and Orson became the ward of Dr Maurice Bernstein, a Chicago physician. Welles graduated from Todd in 1931 and began travelling on an inheritance from his father. After taking a walking and sketching tour of Ireland – he hoped to become a painter – he approached Hilton Edwards of the Gate Theatre, Dublin, with the claim that he was a stage star from New York. After acting in and directing many plays at the Gate and the Gate Studio (Edwards later explained that he didn't believe Welles's claim, but was impressed by his gall), Welles returned to the United States because, as a foreigner, he was not permitted to act in London. Failing to find an acting job in New York, he parlayed introductions from Thornton Wilder and Alexander Woolcott into a role in Katharine Cornell's road company of *Romeo and Juliet*. In 1934 he married Virginia Nicholson, an actress; met Joseph Cotten and John Houseman; directed and appeared in his first film, *The Hearts of Age*; and made his first appearance on radio. He formed the Mercury Theatre with House-man in 1937, after they had produced plays for the Works Progress Administration. His first daughter, Christopher, was born in 1937. *The War of the Worlds*, a Mercury radio broadcast, created a national panic on Halloween 1938. Virginia Nicholson divorced him in 1939; he signed his contract with RKO Radio Pictures the same year. He married Rita Hayworth in 1943 – she divorced him in 1947 – and Paola Mori in 1955. His other children are Rebecca, born in 1944, and Beatrice, born in 1956. Welles now lives in Europe.

Films as Director

The Hearts of Age (1934)

Producer | William Vance
Directors | Orson Welles, William Vance

With Orson Welles, Virginia Nicholson, William Vance.

Filmed (in 16 mm) in Woodstock, Illinois, during the summer of 1934. Running time, approximately 4 min.

Too Much Johnson (1938)

Production Company | Mercury Productions
Producers | Orson Welles, John Houseman
Director | Orson Welles
Assistant Director | John Berry
Script | Orson Welles. Based on the play by William Gillette
Director of Photography | Paul Dunbar

Joseph Cotten (*Johnson*), Virginia Nicholson, Edgar Barrier, Arlene Francis, Ruth Ford, Mary Wickes, Eustace Wyatt, Guy Kingsley, George Duthie, John Berry, Herbert Drake, Marc Blitzstein, Howard Smith.

Filmed (in 16 mm) in New York City and elsewhere in New York during the spring of 1938. Made for a Mercury Theatre stage production of *Too Much Johnson* (Stony Creek Summer Theatre, New York), but never edited or shown publicly. Running time, approximately 40 min. The only copy of this film was destroyed in a fire at Welles's villa in Madrid in August 1970.

In 1939 Welles made a film for use in his vaudeville show *The Green Goddess*, and shot test scenes in Hollywood for *Heart of Darkness*.

Citizen Kane (1941)

Production Company | Mercury Productions
Executive Producer | George J. Schaefer
Producer | Orson Welles
Associate Producer | Richard Barr
Director | Orson Welles
Assistant Director | Richard Wilson
Script | Herman J. Mankiewicz, Orson Welles
Director of Photography | Gregg Toland
Camera Operator | Bert Shipman

167

Editors	Mark Robson, Robert Wise
Art Director	Van Nest Polglase
Associate Art Director	Perry Ferguson
Set Decorator	Darrell Silvera
Special Effects	Vernon L. Walker
Music/Musical Director	Bernard Herrmann
Costumes	Edward Stevenson
Sound Recordists	Bailey Fesler, James G. Stewart

Orson Welles (*Charles Foster Kane*), Joseph Cotten (*Jedediah Leland*; also *Newsreel Reporter*), Everett Sloane (*Bernstein*), Dorothy Comingore (*Susan Alexander Kane*), Ray Collins (*James W. Gettys*), William Alland (*Jerry Thompson*; also *Newsreel Narrator*), Agnes Moorehead (*Mary Kane*), Ruth Warrick (*Emily Norton Kane*), George Coulouris (*Walter Parks Thatcher*), Erskine Sanford (*Herbert Carter*; also *Newsreel Reporter*), Harry Shannon (*Jim Kane*), Philip Van Zandt (*Rawlston*), Paul Stewart (*Raymond*), Fortunio Bonanova (*Matisti*), Georgia Backus (*Miss Anderson, Curator of Thatcher Library*), Buddy Swan (*Charles Foster Kane, aged 8*), Sonny Bupp (*Kane, Jr*), Gus Schilling (*Head Waiter*), Richard Barr (*Hillman*), Joan Blair (*Georgia*), Al Eben (*Mike*), Charles Bennett (*Entertainer*), Milt Kibbee (*Reporter*), Tom Curran (*Teddy Roosevelt*), Irving Mitchell (*Dr Corey*), Edith Evanson (*Nurse*), Arthur Kay (*Orchestra Leader*), Tudor Williams (*Chorus Master*), Herbert Corthell (*City Editor*), Benny Rubin (*Smather*), Edmund Cobb (*Reporter*), Frances Neal (*Ethel*), Robert Dudley (*Photographer*), Ellen Lowe (*Miss Townsend*), Gino Corrado (*Gino, the waiter*), Alan Ladd, Louise Currie, Eddie Coke, Walter Sande, Arthur O'Connell, Katherine Trosper, and Richard Wilson (*Reporters*).

Filmed at the RKO studios in Hollywood, 29 June–23 October 1940. US premiere in New York, 1 May 1941; GB, October 1941. Running time, 119 min.
Distributors: RKO Radio (USA and GB).

The Magnificent Ambersons (1942)

Production Company	Mercury Productions
Executive Producer	George J. Schaefer
Producer	Orson Welles
Director	Orson Welles (additional scenes directed by Freddie Fleck and Robert Wise)
Assistant Director	Freddie Fleck
Script	Orson Welles. Based on the novel by Booth Tarkington
Director of Photography	Stanley Cortez
Additional Photography	Russell Metty, Harry J. Wild
Editors	Robert Wise, Jack Moss, Mark Robson
Art Director	Mark-Lee Kirk
Set Decorator	Al Fields
Special Effects	Vernon L. Walker

Music	Bernard Herrmann
Additional Music	Roy Webb
Costumes	Edward Stevenson
Sound Recordists	Bailey Fesler, James G. Stewart
Narrator	Orson Welles

Tim Holt (*George Amberson Minafer*), Joseph Cotten (*Eugene Morgan*), Dolores Costello (*Isabel Amberson Minafer*), Agnes Moorehead (*Fanny Minafer*), Anne Baxter (*Lucy Morgan*), Ray Collins (*Jack Amberson*), Richard Bennett (*Major Amberson*), Don Dillaway (*Wilbur Minafer*), Erskine Sanford (*Roger Bronson*), J. Louis Johnson (*Sam*), Gus Schilling (*Drugstore Clerk*), Charles Phipps (*Uncle John*), Dorothy Vaughan and Elmer Jerome (*Spectators at funeral*), Olive Ball (*Mary*), Nina Guilbert and John Elliot (*Guests*), Anne O'Neal (*Mrs Foster*), Kathryn Sheldon and Georgia Backus (*Matrons*), Henry Roquemore (*Hardware Man*), Hilda Plowright (*Nurse*), Mel Ford (*Fred Kinney*), Bob Pittard (*Charlie Johnson*), Lillian Nicholson (*Landlady*), Billy Elmer (*House Servant*), Maynard Holmes and Lew Kelly (*Citizens*), Bobby Cooper (*George as a boy*), Drew Roddy (*Elijah*), Jack Baxley (*Reverend Smith*), Heenan Elliott (*Labourer*), Nancy Gates (*Girl*), John Maguire (*Young Man*), Ed Howard (*Chauffeur/Citizen*), William Blees (*Youth at accident*), James Westerfield (*Cop at accident*), Philip Morris (*Cop*), Jack Santoro (*Barber*), Louis Hayward (*Ballroom extra*).

Filmed at the RKO studios in Hollywood, 28 October 1941–22 January 1942. US premiere, 13 August 1942; GB, March 1943. Running time, 88 min. (originally 131 min.).
Distributors: RKO Radio (USA and GB).

It's All True (1942)

Production Company	Mercury Productions, for the Office of the Coordinator of Inter-American Affairs and RKO Radio
Executive Producers	Nelson Rockefeller, George J. Schaefer
Producer	Orson Welles
Associate Producer	Richard Wilson
Director	Orson Welles (and Norman Foster as co-director of the *Bonito* episode)
Script	Orson Welles, Norman Foster, John Fante
Director of Photography	W. Howard Greene
Second Cameraman	Harry J. Wild
Colour Process (*Carnival* episode)	Technicolor
Editor	Joe Noriega

José Olimpio Meira or Jacaré, Tata, Mané, Jeronymo, Sebastião Prata or Grande Otelo, Domingo Soler, Jesús Vasquez.

Filmed on location in Brazil from January to August, 1942. Uncompleted and never shown.

Journey Into Fear (1943)

Production Company	Mercury Productions
Executive Producer	George J. Schaefer
Producer	Orson Welles
Director	Norman Foster (and Orson Welles, uncredited)
Script	Joseph Cotten, Orson Welles. Based on the novel by Eric Ambler
Director of Photography	Karl Struss
Editor	Mark Robson
Art Directors	Albert S. D'Agostino, Mark-Lee Kirk
Set Decorators	Darrell Silvera, Ross Dowd
Special Effects	Vernon L. Walker
Music	Roy Webb
Costumes	Edward Stevenson

Joseph Cotten (*Howard Graham*), Dolores Del Rio (*Josette Martel*), Orson Welles (*Colonel Haki*), Ruth Warrick (*Stephanie Graham*), Agnes Moorehead (*Mrs Mathews*), Everett Sloane (*Kopeikin*), Jack Moss (*Banat*), Jack Durant (*Gogo*), Eustace Wyatt (*Dr Haller*), Frank Readick (*Mathews*), Edgar Barrier (*Kuvetli*), Stefan Schnabel (*Purser*), Hans Conried (*Oo Lang Sang, the magician*), Robert Meltzer (*Steward*), Richard Bennett (*Ship's Captain*), Shifra Haran (*Mrs Haklet*), Herbert Drake, Bill Roberts.

Filmed at the RKO studios in Hollywood, 1942–3. First shown in USA, 12 February 1943; GB, October 1943. Running time, 71 min.
Distributors: RKO Radio (USA and GB).

The Stranger (1946)

Production Company	International Pictures
Producer	S. P. Eagle [Sam Spiegel]
Director	Orson Welles
Assistant Director	Jack Voglin
Script	Anthony Veiller (and John Huston, Orson Welles, uncredited)
Story	Victor Trivas, Decla Dunning
Director of Photography	Russell Metty
Editor	Ernest Nims
Art Director	Perry Ferguson
Music	Bronislaw Kaper
Orchestrations	Harold Byrns, Sidney Cutner
Costumes	Michael Woulfe
Sound	Carson F. Jowett, Arthur Johns

Orson Welles (*Franz Kindler* alias *Professor Charles Rankin*), Loretta Young (*Mary Longstreet*), Edward G. Robinson (*Inspector Wilson*), Philip Merivale (*Judge Longstreet*), Richard Long (*Noah Longstreet*), Byron Keith (*Dr Lawrence*), Billy House (*Mr Potter*), Martha Wentworth (*Sarah*), Konstantin Shayne (*Konrad Meinike*), Theodore Gottlieb (*Farbright*), Pietro Sosso (*Mr Peabody*), Isabel O'Madigan.

Filmed in Hollywood, 1945. First shown in USA, 25 May 1946; GB, 25 August 1946. Running time, 95 min. (85 min. in USA; originally 115 min.).
Distributors: RKO Radio (USA and GB).

In 1946, Welles filmed sequences for use in his play *Around the World*.

The Lady from Shanghai (1946)

Production Company	Columbia
Executive Producer	Harry Cohn
Associate Producers	Richard Wilson, William Castle
Director	Orson Welles
Assistant Director	Sam Nelson
Script	Orson Welles. Freely adapted from the novel *If I Die Before I Wake* by Sherwood King
Director of Photography	Charles Lawton, Jr
Camera Operator	Irving Klein
Editor	Viola Lawrence
Art Directors	Stephen Goosson, Sturges Carne
Set Decorators	Wilbur Menefee, Herman Schoenbrun
Special Effects	Lawrence Butler
Music	Heinz Roemheld
Musical Director	M. W. Stoloff
Orchestrations	Herschel Burke Gilbert
Song 'Please Don't Kiss Me'	Allan Roberts, Doris Fisher
Costumes (gowns)	Jean Louis
Sound	Lodge Cunningham

Orson Welles (*Michael O'Hara*), Rita Hayworth (*Elsa Bannister*), Everett Sloane (*Arthur Bannister*), Glenn Anders (*George Grisby*), Ted de Corsia (*Sidney Broom*), Gus Schilling (*Goldie*), Louis Merrill (*Jake*), Erskine Sanford (*Judge*), Carl Frank (*District Attorney Galloway*), Evelyn Ellis (*Bessie*), Wong Show Chong (*Li*), Harry Shannon (*Horse cab driver*), Sam Nelson (*Captain*), Richard Wilson (*District Attorney's Assistant*), and players of the Mandarin Theatre of San Francisco.

Filmed at Columbia Studios in Hollywood, and on location in Mexico and San Francisco, 1946. First shown in GB, 7 March 1948; USA, May 1948. Running time, 86 min.
Distributors: Columbia (USA and GB).

Macbeth (1948)

Production Company	Mercury Productions. For Republic Pictures.
Executive Producer	Charles K. Feldman
Producer	Orson Welles
Associate Producer	Richard Wilson
Director	Orson Welles
Assistant Director	Jack Lacey
Script	Orson Welles. Adapted from the play by Shakespeare
Dialogue Director	William Alland
Director of Photography	John L. Russell
Second Unit Photographer	William Bradford
Editor	Louis Lindsay
Art Director	Fred Ritter
Set Decorators	John McCarthy, Jr, James Redd
Special Effects	Howard Lydecker, Theodore Lydecker
Music	Jacques Ibert
Musical Director	Efrem Kurtz
Costumes	Orson Welles, Fred Ritter (men's), Adele Palmer (women's)
Make-up	Bob Mark
Sound	John Stransky, Jr, Garry Harris

Orson Welles (*Macbeth*), Jeanette Nolan (*Lady Macbeth*), Dan O'Herlihy (*Macduff*), Edgar Barrier (*Banquo*), Roddy McDowall (*Malcolm*), Erskine Sanford (*Duncan*), Alan Napier (*A Holy Father*), John Dierkes (*Ross*), Keene Curtis (*Lennox*), Peggy Webber (*Lady Macduff/Witch*), Lionel Braham (*Siward*), Archie Heugly (*Young Siward*), Christopher Welles (*Macduff child*), Brainerd Duffield (*1st Murderer/ Witch*), William Alland (*2nd Murderer*), George Chirello (*Seyton*), Gus Schilling (*Porter*), Jerry Farber (*Fleance*), Lurene Tuttle (*Gentlewoman/Witch*), Charles Lederer (*Witch*), Robert Alan (*3rd Murderer*), Morgan Farley (*Doctor*).

Filmed at Republic Studios in Hollywood in twenty-three days during the summer of 1947. First shown in USA, 1 October 1948; GB, 31 May 1951. Running time, 107 min. (later cut to 86 min.).
Distributors: Republic (USA and GB).

In 1950, Welles made a short film, *La Miracle de Saint Anne*, for use in his play *The Unthinking Lobster*.

Othello (1952)

Production Company	Mercury Productions
Producer	Orson Welles

Associate Producers	Giorgio Patti, Julien Derode, with Walter Bedone, Patrice Dali, Rocco Facchini
Director	Orson Welles
Assistant Director	Michael Washinsky
Script	Orson Welles. Based on the play by Shakespeare
Directors of Photography	Anchise Brizzi, G. R. Aldo, George Fanto, with Obadan Troiani, Alberto Fusi
Editors	Jean Sacha, John Shepridge, Renzo Lucidi, William Morton
Art Director	Alexandre Trauner
Music	Francesco Lavagnino, Alberto Barberis
Musical Director	Willy Ferrero
Costumes	Maria de Matteis
Sound Recordist	Piscitrelli
Narrator	Orson Welles

Orson Welles (*Othello*), Micheál MacLiammóir (*Iago*), Suzanne Cloutier (*Desdemona*), Robert Coote (*Roderigo*), Michael Lawrence (*Cassio*), Hilton Edwards (*Brabantio*), Fay Compton (*Emilia*), Nicholas Bruce (*Lodovico*), Jean Davis (*Montano*), Doris Dowling (*Bianca*), Joseph Cotten (*Senator*), Joan Fontaine (*Page*).

Filmed at the Scalera studios in Rome, and on locations in Morocco (Mogador, Safi, and Mazagan) and Italy (Venice, Tuscany, Rome, Viterbo, Perugia, and the island of Torcello), from 1949 to 1952. First shown at the Cannes Film Festival, 10 May 1952; USA, June 1955; GB, 24 February 1956. Running time, 91 min.
Distributors: United Artists (USA and GB).

Don Quixote (begun in 1955)

Producers	Oscar Dancigers, Orson Welles
Director	Orson Welles
Assistant Director	Paola Mori
Script	Orson Welles. Based on the novel by Miguel de Cervantes
Director of Photography	Jack Draper
Assistant Cameraman	Orson Welles
Narrator	Orson Welles

Francisco Reiguera (*Don Quixote*), Akim Tamiroff (*Sancho Panza*), Patty McCormack (*A girl*; *Dulcinea*), Orson Welles (*Himself*).

Filmed in Mexico (Puebla, Tepozlan, Texcoco, Rio Frio, Mexico City) and in Paris. Running time, approximately 90 min. Uncompleted.

Mr Arkadin [British title: *Confidential Report*] (1955)

Production Company	Cervantes Film Organisation, Sevilla Studios (Spain)/Film Organisation (France). A Mercury Production
Executive Producer	Louis Dolivet
Production Manager	Michel J. Boisrond
Director	Orson Welles
Assistant Directors	José María Ochoa, José Luis De la Serna, Isidoro Martínez Ferri
Script	Orson Welles. Based on his own novel
Director of Photography	Jean Bourgoin
Editor	Renzo Lucidi
Art Director	Orson Welles
Music	Paul Misraki
Costumes	Orson Welles
Sound	Jacques Lebreton
Sound Recordist	Jacques Carrère
Narrator	Orson Welles

Orson Welles (*Gregory Arkadin*), Paola Mori (*Raina Arkadin*), Robert Arden (*Guy Van Stratten*), Akim Tamiroff (*Jacob Zouk*), Michael Redgrave (*Burgomil Trebitsch*), Patricia Medina (*Mily*), Mischa Auer (*The Professor*), Katina Paxinou (*Sophie*), Jack Watling (*Marquis of Rutleigh*), Grégoire Aslan (*Bracco*), Peter Van Eyck (*Thaddeus*), Suzanne Flon (*Baroness Nagel*), Tamara Shane (*Woman in apartment*), Frédéric O'Brady (*Oskar*).

Filmed in France, Spain, Germany, and Italy during eight months of 1954. First shown in GB, 11 August 1955; USA, 11 October 1962. Running time, 100 min.
Distributors: Warner Bros. (GB), Dan Talbot (USA).

Touch of Evil (1958)

Production Company	Universal
Producer	Albert Zugsmith
Production Manager	F. D. Thompson
Director	Orson Welles (additional scenes directed by Harry Keller)
Assistant Directors	Phil Bowles, Terry Nelson
Script	Orson Welles. Freely adapted from the novel *Badge of Evil* by Whit Masterson
Director of Photography	Russell Metty
Editors	Virgil W. Vogel, Aaron Stell

Art Directors	Alexander Golitzen, Robert Clatworthy
Set Decorators	Russell A. Gausman, John P. Austin
Music	Henry Mancini
Musical Supervisor	Joseph Gershenson
Costumes	Bill Thomas
Sound	Leslie I. Carey, Frank Wilkinson

Orson Welles (*Hank Quinlan*), Charlton Heston (*Ramon Miguel 'Mike' Vargas*), Janet Leigh (*Susan Vargas*), Joseph Calleia (*Pete Menzies*), Akim Tamiroff ('*Uncle Joe' Grande*), Valentin De Vargas (*Pancho*), Ray Collins (*District Attorney Adair*), Dennis Weaver (*Motel Clerk*), Joanna Moore (*Marcia Linnekar*), Mort Mills (*Schwartz*), Marlene Dietrich (*Tanya*), Victor Millan (*Manolo Sanchez*), Lalo Rios (*Risto*), Michael Sargent (*Pretty Boy*), Mercedes McCambridge (*Gang Leader*), Joseph Cotten (*Detective*), Zsa Zsa Gabor (*Owner of strip joint*), Phil Harvey (*Blaine*), Joi Lansing (*Blonde*), Harry Shannon (*Gould*), Rusty Wescoatt (*Casey*), Wayne Taylor, Ken Miller, and Raymond Rodriguez (*Gang Members*), Arlene McQuade (*Ginnie*), Domenick Delgarde (*Lackey*), Joe Basulto (*Young Delinquent*), Jennie Dias (*Jackie*), Yolanda Bojorquez (*Bobbie*), Eleanor Dorado (*Lia*).

Filmed at Universal Studios in Hollywood and on location at Venice, California during the winter of 1957–8. First shown in USA, February 1958; GB, 1 May 1958. Running time, 93 min.
Distributors: Universal (USA), Rank (GB).

The Trial (1962)

Production Company	Paris Europa Productions (Paris)/FI-C-IT (Rome)/Hisa-Films (Munich)
Producers	Alexander Salkind, Michael Salkind
Production Manager	Robert Florat
Director	Orson Welles
Assistant Directors	Marc Maurette, Paul Seban, Sophie Becker
Script	Orson Welles. Based on the novel *Der Prozess* by Franz Kafka
Director of Photography	Edmond Richard
Camera Operator	Adolphe Charlet
Editors	Yvonne Martin, Denise Baby, Fritz Mueller
Art Director	Jean Mandaroux
Music	Jean Ledrut, and the Adagio for Organ and Strings by Tomaso Albinoni
Costumes	Hélène Thibault
Sound	Jacques Lebreton
Sound Recordists	Julien Coutellier, Guy Villette
Pin-screen prologue	Alexandre Alexeieff, Claire Parker
Narrator	Orson Welles

Anthony Perkins (*Joseph K.*), Orson Welles (*Hastler*), Jeanne Moreau (*Miss Burstner*), Romy Schneider (*Leni*), Elsa Martinelli (*Hilda*), Suzanne Flon (*Miss Pittl*), Madeleine Robinson (*Mrs Grubach*), Akim Tamiroff (*Block*), Arnoldo Foà (*Inspector*), Fernand Ledoux (*Clerk of the Court*), Maurice Teynac (*Director of K.'s office*), Billy Kearns (*1st Police Officer*), Jess Hahn (*2nd Police Officer*), William Chappell (*Titorelli*), Raoul Delfosse, Karl Studer, and Jean-Claude Remoleux (*Executioners*), Wolfgang Reichmann (*Usher*), Thomas Holtzmann (*Student*), Maydra Shore (*Irmie*), Max Haufler (*Uncle Max*), Michel Lonsdale (*Priest*), Max Buchsbaum (*Judge*), Van Doude (*Archivist in cut scenes*), Katina Paxinou (*Scientist in cut scenes*).

Filmed at Studio de Boulogne, Paris, at the Gare d'Orsay, and in Zagreb, 26 March– 2 June 1962. First shown in Paris, 21 December 1962; GB, 14 November 1963; USA, 20 February 1963. Running time, 120 min. (118 min. in English version). Distributors: UFA-Comacico (France), BLC/British Lion (GB), Astor (USA). French title: LE PROCÈS

Chimes at Midnight (1966)

Production Company	Internacional Films Española (Madrid)/Alpine (Basle)
Executive Producer	Alessandro Tasca
Producers	Emiliano Piedra, Angel Escolano
Production Manager	Gustavo Quintana
Director	Orson Welles
Second Unit Director	Jesús Franco
Assistant Directors	Tony Fuentes, Juan Cobos
Script	Orson Welles. Adapted from the plays *Richard II*, *Henry IV Parts I and II*, *Henry V*, and *The Merry Wives of Windsor* by William Shakespeare, and (for the commentary) *The Chronicles of England* by Raphael Holinshed
Director of Photography	Edmond Richard
Camera Operator	Adolphe Charlet
Second Unit Photographer	Alejandro Ulloa
Editor	Fritz Mueller
Art Directors	José Antonio de la Guerra, Mariano Erdorza
Music	Angelo Francesco Lavagnino
Musical Director	Carlo Franci
Costumes	Orson Welles
Sound Recordist	Peter Parasheles
Narrator	Ralph Richardson

Orson Welles (*Sir John Falstaff*), Keith Baxter (*Prince Hal, later King Henry V*), John Gielgud (*King Henry IV*), Jeanne Moreau (*Doll Tearsheet*), Margaret

Rutherford (*Mistress Quickly*), Norman Rodway (*Henry Percy, called Hotspur*), Marina Vlady (*Kate Percy*), Alan Webb (*Justice Shallow*), Walter Chiari (*Silence*), Michael Aldridge (*Pistol*), Tony Beckley (*Poins*), Fernando Rey (*Worcester*), Andrew Faulds (*Westmoreland*), José Nieto (*Northumberland*), Jeremy Rowe (*Prince John*), Beatrice Welles (*Falstaff's Page*), Paddy Bedford (*Bardolph*), Julio Peña, Fernando Hilbert, Andrés Mejuto, Keith Pyott, Charles Farrell.

Filmed in Barcelona, Madrid, and other Spanish locations, Winter 1964–Spring 1965. First shown at Cannes Film Festival, 8 May 1966; USA, 19 March 1967; GB, 23 March 1967. Running time, 119 min. (115 min. in GB).
Distributors: Planet (GB), Peppercorn-Wormser (USA).
Spanish title: CAMPANADAS A MEDIANOCHE; US title: FALSTAFF

The Immortal Story (1968)

Production Company	ORTF/Albina Films
Producer	Micheline Rozan
Production Manager	Marc Maurette
Director	Orson Welles
Assistant Directors	Olivier Gérard, Tony Fuentes, Patrice Torok
Script	Orson Welles. Based on the novella by Isak Dinesen [Karen Blixen]
Director of Photography	Willy Kurant
Colour Process	Eastman Colour
Assistant Cameramen	Jean Orjollet, Jacques Assuerds
Editors	Yolande Maurette, Marcelle Pluet, Françoise Garnault, Claude Farny
Art Director	André Piltant
Music	piano pieces by Erik Satie, played by Aldo Ciccolini and Jean-Joel Barbier
Costumes (for Jeanne Moreau)	Pierre Cardin
Sound	Jean Neny
Narrator	Orson Welles

Orson Welles (*Mr Clay*), Jeanne Moreau (*Virginie Ducrot*), Roger Coggio (*Elishama Levinsky*), Norman Eshley (*Paul*), Fernando Rey (*Merchant*).

Filmed in Paris and Madrid, September–November 1966. First shown on French television simultaneously with its theatrical premiere in France, 24 May 1968; USA, New York Film Festival, 18 September 1968; GB, 3 April 1969 (previously at London Film Festival, 29 November 1968). Running time, 58 min.
Distributors: Hunter Films (GB), Altura Films (USA).
French title: HISTOIRE IMMORTELLE

The Deep (1970)

Director	Orson Welles
Script	Orson Welles. Based on the novel *Dead Calm* by Charles Williams
Director of Photography	Willy Kurant
Colour Process	Eastman Colour

Orson Welles (*Russ Brewer*), Jeanne Moreau (*Ruth Warriner*), Laurence Harvey (*Hughie Warriner*), Olga Palinkas (*Rae Ingram*), Michael Bryant (*John Ingram*).

Filmed off the Dalmatian coast at Hvar, Yugoslavia, 1967–9.

The Other Side of the Wind (1972)

Director	Orson Welles
Script	Orson Welles
Director of Photography	Gary Graver
Colour Process	Eastman Colour

Filming began 23 August 1970 in Los Angeles.

Film performances

1934   The Hearts of Age (as Death. *d*: Orson Welles, William Vance)

1940   The Swiss Family Robinson (as Narrator. *d*: Edward Ludwig)

1941   Citizen Kane (as Charles Foster Kane. *d*: Orson Welles)

1942   The Magnificent Ambersons (as Narrator. *d*: Orson Welles)

1943   Journey Into Fear (as Colonel Haki. *d*: Norman Foster, Orson Welles)
       Jane Eyre (as Edward Rochester. *d*: Robert Stevenson)

1944   Follow the Boys (as Himself. *d*: Edward Sutherland)

1945   Tomorrow is Forever (as John Macdonald. *d*: Irving Pichel)

1946   The Stranger (as Franz Kindler alias Professor Charles Rankin. *d*: Orson Welles)
       The Lady from Shanghai (as Michael O'Hara. *d*: Orson Welles)
       Duel in the Sun (as Narrator. *d*: King Vidor)

1947   Black Magic (as Cagliostro. *d*: Gregory Ratoff)

1948   Macbeth (as Macbeth. *d*: Orson Welles)
       Prince of Foxes (as Cesare Borgia. *d*: Henry King)

1949   The Third Man (as Harry Lime. *d*: Carol Reed)

1950   The Black Rose (as General Bayan. *d*: Henry Hathaway)

1952   Othello (as Othello. *d*: Orson Welles)

1953   Trent's Last Case (as Sigsbee Manderson. *d*: Herbert Wilcox)
       Si Versailles m'était conté/Versailles (as Benjamin Franklin. *d:* Sacha Guitry)
       L'Uomo, la Bestia e la Virtù (as The Beast. *d:* Steno [Stefano Vanzina])

1954   Napoleon (as Hudson Lowe. *d:* Sacha Guitry)
       Three Cases of Murder (as Lord Mountdrago in the episode directed by George More O'Ferrall)

1955   Mr Arkadin/Confidential Report (as Gregory Arkadin and Narrator. *d:* Orson Welles)
       Trouble in the Glen (as Sanin Cejador y Mengues. *d*: Herbert Wilcox)
       Don Quixote (as Himself and Narrator. *d*: Orson Welles)

1956   Moby Dick (as Father Mapple. *d*: John Huston)

1957   Man in the Shadow/Pay the Devil (as Virgil Renckler. *d*: Jack Arnold)
        The Long Hot Summer (as Varner. *d*: Martin Ritt)

1958   Touch of Evil (as Hank Quinlan. *d*: Orson Welles)
        The Roots of Heaven (as Cy Sedgwick. *d*: John Huston)
        The Vikings (as Narrator. *d*: Richard Fleischer)

1959   Compulsion (as Jonathan Wilk. *d*: Richard Fleischer)
        David e Golia/David and Goliath (as Saul. *d*: Richard Pottier, Ferdinando Baldi)
        Ferry to Hong Kong (as Captain Hart. *d*: Lewis Gilbert)

1960   Austerlitz (as Fulton. *d*: Abel Gance)
        Crack in the Mirror (as Hagolin and Lamorcière. *d*: Richard Fleischer)
        I Tartari/The Tartars (as Burundai. *d*: Richard Thorpe)

1961   King of Kings (as Narrator. *d*: Nicholas Ray)
        Lafayette (as Benjamin Franklin. *d*: Jean Dréville)

1962   The Trial/Le Procès (as Hastler. *d*: Orson Welles)
        RoGoPaG (as The Director in the episode *La Ricotta* directed by Pier Paolo Pasolini)

1964   La Fabuleuse Aventure de Marco Polo/The Fabulous Adventures of Marco Polo (GB)/Marco the Magnificent! (US) (as Ackermann. *d*: Denys de la Patellière, Noël Howard)

1965   Paris brûle-t-il?/Is Paris Burning? (as Consul Raoul Nordling. *d*: René Clément)
        Treasure Island (as Long John Silver. *d*: Jesús Franco; unfinished)

1966   Chimes at Midnight/Campanadas a Medianoche (as Sir John Falstaff. *d*: Orson Welles)
        The Sailor from Gibraltar (as Louis from Mozambique. *d*: Tony Richardson)
        A Man for All Seasons (as Cardinal Wolsey. *d*: Fred Zinnemann)

1967   The Immortal Story/Histoire Immortelle (as Mr Clay and Narrator. *d*: Orson Welles)
        Casino Royale (as Le Chiffre in the episode directed by Joseph McGrath)
        I'll Never Forget What's'isname (as Jonathan Lute. *d*: Michael Winner)
        Oedipus the King (as Tiresias. *d*: Philip Saville)

1968   House of Cards (as Charles Leschenhaut. *d*: John Guillermin)
        L'Etoile du Sud/The Southern Star (as Plankett. *d*: Sidney Hayers)

1969   Bitka na Neretvi/The Battle of the River Neretva (as Senator. *d*: Veljko Bulajic)
        Mihai Viteazu/Michael the Brave (*d*: Sergiu Nicolaescu)

Tepepa (as Colonel Cascorro. *d*: Giulio Petroni)
Una su Tredici/Twelve Plus One (as Markau. *d*: Nicolas Gessner)
The Kremlin Letter (as Aleksei Bresnavitch. *d*: John Huston)
Start the Revolution Without Me (as Himself and Narrator. *d*: Bud Yorkin)

1970   Catch-22 (as General Dreedle. *d*: Mike Nichols)
Waterloo (as Louis XVIII. *d*: Sergei Bondarchuk)
The Deep (as Russ Brewer. *d*: Orson Welles)
Upon This Rock (as Michelangelo. *d*: Harry Rasky)

1971   A Safe Place (*d*: Henry Jaglom)
The Toy Factory (*d*: Bert Gordon)
Get to Know Your Rabbit (*d*: Brian de Palma)
La Décade Prodigieuse (as Theo Van Horn. *d*: Claude Chabrol)
The Canterbury Tales (as Old January. *d*: Pier Paolo Pasolini)
To Kill a Stranger (*d*: Peter Collinson)

Welles also appeared in the documentary short *Désordre* (*Disorder*, *d*: Jacques Baratier, 1950), and appeared in (as himself) and narrated a short feature, *Return to Glennascaul*, directed by Hilton Edwards in Ireland in 1951.

He was narrator for the documentary films *Out of Darkness* (1955, *d*: Albert Wassermann), *Les Seigneurs de la Forêt* (Belgium, 1958, *d*: Heinz Sielmann, Henry Brandt. co-narrator: William Warfield), *South Seas Adventure* (1958, *d*: Carl Dudley *et al.*), *High Journey* (France, 1959, for NATO. *d*: Peter Baylis), *Der Grosser Atlantik* (*River of the Ocean*, West Germany, 1962, *d*: Peter Baylis), *The Finest Hours* (1964, *d*: Peter Baylis), *A King's Story* (1965, *d*: Harry Booth), *Barbed Water* (1969, *d*: Adrian J. Wensley-Walker), *Sentinels of Silence* (Mexico, 1971, *d*: Robert Amran), and *Directed by John Ford* (1971, *d*: Peter Bogdanovich). He recorded the commentary for *The Spanish Earth* (1937, *d*: Joris Ivens), but was superseded as narrator by Ernest Hemingway.

Theatre

Welles made his first stage appearance at the age of three, when he played Madame Butterfly's love-child at the Opera House in Ravinia, Illinois. He played several other juvenile roles at the Chicago Opera House, and appeared as Peter Rabbit in an Easter pageant at Marshall Field's department store in Chicago. He began staging plays for his family and friends at an early age; when he was nine he did a one-man version of *King Lear*. Other plays he presented with puppets, supplying voices for all the characters. In 1925, when he was ten, he appeared in several plays at the Washington Grade School in Madison, Wisconsin, including *A Christmas Carol* (as Scrooge). In the summer of 1925 he produced a one-man show of *Dr Jekyll and Mr Hyde* at Camp Indianola. At the Todd School in Woodstock, Illinois, which he entered in the autumn of 1926, he put on a Halloween magic show and appeared in a Nativity play (as the Blessed Virgin), as Christ in *The Servant in the House*, and as Judas in *Dust of the Road*. Under the tutelage of Roger Hill during his five years at the Todd School, Welles also directed and acted in about thirty other plays, including *Julius Caesar*, *Richard III*, a condensed version of the Falstaff cycle (which he later filmed as *Chimes at Midnight*), and *Androcles and the Lion*.

Stage productions

1931   *The Lady from the Sea* by Henrik Ibsen (Dublin Gate Theatre Studio)
The Three Sisters by Anton Chekhov (Dublin Gate Theatre Studio)
Alice in Wonderland USA (Dublin Gate Theatre Studio)

1934   *Trilby* by Gerald du Maurier (Todd School, Woodstock, Illinois)
The Drunkard by Mr Smith of Boston (Todd School, Woodstock, Illinois)
Hamlet by William Shakespeare (Todd School, Woodstock, Illinois)
Czar Paul by Dimitri Merejewski (Todd School, Woodstock, Illinois)

1936   *Macbeth* by William Shakespeare (Negro People's Theatre production for the Federal Theatre at Lafayette Theatre, Harlem)
Turpentine by A. Smith and P. Morell (Negro People's Theatre production for the Federal Theatre at Lafayette Theatre, Harlem)
Horse Eats Hat adapted by Welles and E. Denby from Labiche's *Un Chapeau de Paille d'Italie* (Federal Theatre, at Maxine Elliott Theatre, New York)

1937   *Dr Faustus* by Christopher Marlowe (Federal Theatre at Maxine Elliott Theatre, New York)
Julius Caesar by William Shakespeare (Mercury Theatre at Comedy Theatre, New York; later at National Theatre, New York)
The Cradle Will Rock by Marc Blitzstein (Mercury Theatre at Venice Theatre, New York)

1938   *The Shoemaker's Holiday* by Thomas Dekker (Mercury Theatre at Comedy Theatre, New York)
Heartbreak House by George Bernard Shaw (Mercury Theatre at Comedy Theatre, New York)
Too Much Johnson adapted by Welles from William Gillette (Stony Creek Summer Theatre, New York)
The Importance of Being Earnest by Oscar Wilde (Cape Playhouse, Dennis, Mass.)
Danton's Death by Georg Büchner (Mercury Theatre at Comedy Theatre, New York)

1939   *Five Kings* adapted by Welles from Shakespeare's *Henry IV Parts I and II, Henry V, Henry VI Parts I-III, Richard II* and *Richard III* (Theatre Guild at Colonial Theatre, Boston)
The Green Goddess adapted by Welles from William Archer (R.K.O. Vaudeville circuit)

1941   *Native Son* by Paul Green and Richard Wright (Mercury Theatre at St James Theatre, New York)

1942   *Mercury Wonder Show* (played for troops in circus tent, Cahuenga Boulevard, Los Angeles)

1946   *Around the World* adapted by Welles and Cole Porter from Jules Verne (Adelphi Theatre, New York)

1947 *Macbeth* by William Shakespeare (Utah Centennial Festival, Salt Lake City)

1950 *Time Runs* adapted by Welles from *Faust* (Théâtre Edouard VII, Paris, and on tour in West Germany. The programme also contained a scene from *The Importance of Being Earnest* and a scene from *Henry VI, Part I*) *Une Grosse Légume/The Unthinking Lobster* adapted by Welles from his own novel (Théâtre Edouard VII, Paris)

1951 *Othello* by William Shakespeare (St James's Theatre, London)

1953 *The Lady in the Ice*, ballet written and designed by Welles (Ballet de Paris at Stoll Theatre, London)

1955 *Moby Dick – Rehearsed* adapted by Welles from Herman Melville (Duke of York's Theatre, London)

1956 *King Lear* by William Shakespeare (City Center, New York)

1960 *Chimes at Midnight* adapted by Welles from Shakespeare (Grand Opera House, Belfast) *Rhinoceros* by Eugène Ionesco (Royal Court Theatre, London)

Stage performances

1931 *The Jew Süss* by Leon Feuchtwanger (as Duke Alexander of Wurtemburg. Dublin Gate Theatre)
The Dead Ride Fast by David Sears (as Ralph Bentley. Dublin Gate Theatre)
The Archduke by Percy Robinson (as General Bazaine. Dublin Gate Theatre)
Mogu of the Desert by Padraic O'Conaire (as The Grand Vizier. Dublin Gate Theatre)

1932 *Death Takes a Holiday* by Alberto Casella (as Duke Lamberto. Dublin Gate Theatre)
Hamlet by William Shakespeare (as The Ghost and Fortinbras. Dublin Gate Theatre)
The Circle by Somerset Maugham (as Lord Porteus. Abbey Theatre, Dublin)

At the Dublin Gate and Abbey Theatres, Welles also played minor roles in *Timon of Athens*, *King John* and *Richard III* (Shakespeare); *The Devil* (Benn W. Levy); *Grumpy* (Horace Hodges and T. Wigney Percyval); *The Emperor Jones* (Eugene O'Neill); *The Father* (August Strindberg); *Peer Gynt* (Henrik Ibsen); *Mr Wu* (Harry M. Vernon and Harold Owen); *Dr Knock* (Jules Romains); *La Locandiera* (Carlo Goldoni); *The Rivals* (Richard Brinsley Sheridan); *The Play's the Thing* (Ferenc Molnar); *The Makropoulos Secret* (Karel Capek); *Man and Superman* (George Bernard Shaw); *Volpone* (Ben Jonson); and *The Dover Road* (A. A. Milne).

1933–4 With Katharine Cornell's touring company in the USA:
The Barretts of Wimpole Street by Rudolph Besier (as Octavius Barrett)

Romeo and Juliet by William Shakespeare (as Mercutio)
Candida by George Bernard Shaw (as Marchbanks)

1934   *Trilby* by George du Maurier (as Svengali. Todd School, Woodstock, Illinois)
Hamlet by William Shakespeare (as Claudius. Todd School, Woodstock, Illinois)
Czar Paul by Dimitri Merejewski (as Count Pahlen. Todd School, Woodstock, Illinois)
Romeo and Juliet by William Shakespeare (as Chorus and Tybalt. Katharine Cornell Company at Martin Beck Theatre, New York)

1935   *Panic* by Archibald MacLeish (as McGafferty. Phoenix Theatre Group at Imperial Theatre, New York)

1936   *Ten Million Ghosts* by Sidney Kingsley (as André Pequot. St James Theatre, New York)

1937   *Dr Faustus* by Christopher Marlowe (as Faustus. Federal Theatre at Maxine Elliott Theatre, New York)
Julius Caesar by William Shakespeare (as Brutus. Mercury Theatre at Century Theatre, New York)

1938   *Heartbreak House* by George Bernard Shaw (as Captain Shotover. Mercury Theatre at Comedy Theatre, New York)
Danton's Death by Georg Büchner (as Saint-Just. Mercury Theatre at Comedy Theatre, New York)

1939   *Five Kings* adapted by Welles from Shakespeare (as Falstaff and Richard III. Theatre Guild at Colonial Theatre, Boston)
The Green Goddess adapted by Welles from William Archer (as The Rajah. RKO Vaudeville circuit)

1946   *Around the World* adapted by Welles and Cole Porter from Jules Verne (as Dick Fix. Adelphi Theatre, New York)

1947   *Macbeth* by William Shakespeare (as Macbeth. Utah Centennial Festival, Salt Lake City)

1950   *Time Runs* adapted by Welles from *Faust* (as Dr Faustus. Théâtre Edouard VII, Paris, and on tour of West Germany. The programme also contained a scene from *The Importance of Being Earnest* and a scene from *Henry VI, Part I*)
Une Grosse Légume/The Unthinking Lobster adapted by Welles from his own novel (as Jake. Théâtre Edouard VII, Paris)

1951   *Othello* by William Shakespeare (as Othello. St James's Theatre, London)

1955   *Moby Dick – Rehearsed* adapted by Welles from Herman Melville (as The Actor Manager, Captain Ahab and Father Mapple; also as King Lear. Duke of York's Theatre, London)

1956   *King Lear* by William Shakespeare (as Lear. City Center, New York)

184

1960   *Chimes at Midnight* adapted by Welles from Shakespeare (as Falstaff. Grand Opera House, Belfast)

Radio

(This listing, probably incomplete, was compiled by Marie Garness as part of her University of Wisconsin master's thesis on Welles's radio work.)

1934–5   Acted in *The March of Time* series (NBC).

1936   Played McGafferty in a condensed version of *Panic* by Archibald MacLeish (CBS); narrated the *Musical Reveries* series (CBS).

1936–7   Narrated and played The Great McCoy in *The Wonder Show* series (Mutual).

1937   Played Lamont Cranston in the crime series *The Shadow* (CBS); acted in *Parted on Her Bridal Tour* (Mutual); adapted, directed, and played Jean Valjean in *Les Misérables* (Mutual).

1938   Acted in *Air Raid* (CBS); adapted, narrated, directed, and acted in the *First Person Singular* series (CBS) from 11 July to 5 September. (The casts for this and subsequent Welles series were largely composed of Mercury Theatre actors, including Joseph Cotten, Agnes Moorehead, Everett Sloane, Ray Collins, Paul Stewart, Erskine Sanford, and Richard Wilson. Bernard Herrmann was musical director, and scriptwriters included Howard Koch, Richard Brooks, Abraham Polonsky, and Herman J. Mankiewicz.) The programmes in the *First Person Singular* series were *Dracula*, *Treasure Island*, *A Tale of Two Cities*, *The Thirty-Nine Steps*, *Three Short Stories* ('I'm a Fool', 'Open Window', and 'My Little Boy'), *Hamlet*, *The Affairs of Anatole*, *The Count of Monte Cristo*, and *The Man Who Was Thursday*. Welles adapted, narrated, directed, and acted in *The Mercury Theatre on the Air* series (CBS) from 11 September to 4 December. The programmes were *Julius Caesar* (with narration from Plutarch by H. V. Kaltenborn), *Jane Eyre*, *Sherlock Holmes*, *Oliver Twist*, *Hell on Ice*, *Seventeen*, *Around the World in Eighty Days*, *The War of the Worlds*, *Heart of Darkness*, *The Gift of the Magi*, *Life with Father*, *The Bishop Murder Case*, *The Pickwick Papers*, *Clarence*, and *The Bridge of San Luis Rey*.

1938–40   Adapted, narrated, directed, and acted in *The Campbell Playhouse* series (CBS) from 9 December 1938 to 2 June 1939, and from 10 September 1939 to 31 March 1940. The programmes were *Rebecca*, with Margaret Sullavan; *Call It a Day*, with Bea Lillie and Jane Wyatt; *A Christmas Carol*; *A Farewell to Arms*, with Katharine Hepburn; *Counsellor at Law*, with Gertrude Berg; *Mutiny on the Bounty*; *The Chicken Wagon Family*, with Burgess Meredith; *I Lost My Girlish Laughter*, with Ilka Chase; *Arrowsmith*, with Helen Hayes; *The Green Goddess*, with Madeleine Carroll; *Burlesque*, with Sam Levine; *State Fair*; *The Royal Regiment*, with Mary Astor; *The Glass Key*; *Beau Geste*; *Twentieth Century*; *Show Boat*, with Edna Ferber, Helen Morgan, and Margaret Sullavan; *Les Misérables*, with Walter Huston; *The Patriot*, with Anna May Wong; *Private Lives*, with Gertrude Lawrence; *Black Daniel*, with Joan Bennett; *Wickford Point*; *Our Town*; *The Bad Man*, with Ida Lupino; *American Cavalcade*, with Cornelia Otis Skinner; *Victoria Regina*, with Helen Hayes; *Peter Ibbetson*, with Helen Hayes; *The Count of Monte Cristo*; *Algiers*, with Paulette Goddard; *Escape*, with Wendy Barrie; *Liliom*, with Helen Hayes; *The Magnificent Ambersons*, with Walter Huston; *The Hurricane*, with Mary Astor; *The Murder of Roger Ackroyd*, with Edna May Oliver; *The Garden of Allah*, with Claudette Colbert; *Dodsworth*, with Fay Bainter; *Lost Horizon*, with Sigrid Gurie; *Vanessa*; *There's Always a Woman*, with Marie Wilson; *A Christmas Carol*, with Lionel Barrymore; *Come and Get It*; *Becky Sharp*, with Helen Hayes; *This Lonely Heart*, with Bette Davis; *The Citadel*, with Miriam Hopkins; *Broome Stages*, with Helen Hayes; *Mr Deeds Goes to Town*, with Gertrude Lawrence; *Dinner at Eight*, with Lucille Ball and Hedda Hopper; *Only Angels Have Wings*, with Joan Blondell; *Rabble in Arms*, with Frances Dee; *Craig's Wife*, with Fay Bainter; *Adventures of Huckleberry Finn*, with Jackie Cooper; *June Moon*, with Jack Benny; and *Jane Eyre*, with Madeleine Carroll.

1941   Directed and narrated his own play, *His Honor, the Mayor*, for *The Free Company* series (CBS).

1941–2   Directed and appeared in *The Lady Esther Show* and *The Orson Welles Almanac* (CBS).

1942   Directed and narrated *Columbus Day*, a play by Welles, R. Metzer, and Norris Houghton, on the *Cavalcade of America* series (CBS).

1942–3   *Hello Americans*, a two-part political series (CBS); *Orson Welles Air Drama*, two programmes (CBS).

1943   Played a crusading editor in an episode of the *Nazi Eyes on Canada* series (Canadian Broadcasting Co.); appeared on the Jack Benny show (NBC).

1944   Political broadcasts for ABC and in the *Socony Vacuum* series (CBS).

1945   Repeat of *The Mercury Theatre on the Air* programmes (CBS); talks on miscellaneous subjects (WJZ, New York); adapted, narrated, directed, and acted in the *This Is My Best* series (CBS) from 13 March to 24 April. The programmes were *Heart of Darkness*, *Miss Dilly Says No*, *Snow White*, *A Diamond as Big as the Ritz*, *The Master of Ballantrae*, *Don't Catch Me*, and *Anything Can Happen*.

1947 Repeat of *The Mercury Theatre on the Air* programmes (CBS); political broadcasts (ABC).

1951 Narrated and played Harry Lime in *The Adventures of Harry Lime* series (BBC), for which he also wrote some of the scripts.

1952 Narrated and acted in the Scotland Yard series *The Black Museum* (BBC); played Moriarty in *Sherlock Holmes* (BBC).

1953 Read Walt Whitman's *Song of Myself* (BBC).

Television

1953 *King Lear* (as Lear. Directed by Peter Brook for CBS).

1955 *The Orson Welles Sketchbook* (Six programmes for BBC); *Around the World with Orson Welles* (series of half-hour programmes for Associated Rediffusion, London – not completed).

1956 Played Oscar Jaffe in *Twentieth Century* by Ben Hecht and Charles MacArthur (Ford Star Jubilee, CBS).

1957 Played in abridged versions of *The Merchant of Venice, Macbeth, Othello*, and *King Lear* (CBS and NBC); narrated *The Fall of the City* by Archibald MacLeish.

1958 Wrote, produced, directed and narrated *The Fountain of Youth*, adapted from a short story by John Collier (Colgate Theatre); directed *The Method* (documentary on the Actors' Studio, for BBC).

1960 Storyteller for *An Arabian Night* (Associated Rediffusion, London).

1961 Wrote, directed and narrated a film on bullfighting for *Tempo* (ABC, London).

1967 Narrated *Ten Days That Shook the World* (Granada, Manchester).

1967–71 Made numerous appearances on *The Dean Martin Show* (NBC).

1969 Directed, wrote, and appeared in *Around the World with Orson Welles* (CBS, as yet unshown); acted as host for a CBS special on Mike Todd; directed films for Italian television.

1970 Storyteller for *To Build a Fire* by Jack London (BBC).

1970–1 Appeared on *The Frost Report* (New York, syndicated) and served as guest host for a week; made three 90-minute appearances on *The Dick Cavett Show* (ABC); narrated an episode of *The Name of the Game* (NBC); spoofed *The War of the Worlds* on *Rowan and Martin's Laugh-In* (NBC); served as host for a series of silent films, *The Silent Years* (WNET, New York).

1971 Appeared on *The Marty Feldman Comedy Machine* (ATV, London).

Welles has also provided the background voice for a number of television commercials. In 1955, he began shooting a television film of his play *Moby Dick – Rehearsed*, but stopped after one day. He also began shooting a television documentary about Gina Lollobrigida in 1958, which was never completed. In 1967, James MacAllen produced and directed a two-part documentary on Welles, *Citizen Welles*, for the CBS *Camera Three* series; and in the same year Welles was the subject of a film made for French television by François Reichenbach.

Welles as Writer

A. Books by Welles

1. *Everybody's Shakespeare*, The Todd Press, Woodstock, Illinois, 1934, including *The Merchant of Venice, Twelfth Night*, and *Julius Caesar*, edited by Welles and Roger Hill, with preface by Welles and Hill and illustrations by Welles.
2. *The Mercury Shakespeare*, Harper and Bros., London and New York, 1939. Revision of the above, with *Macbeth* and an article by Welles added. All four of the plays were also issued in acting editions edited by Welles, 1934–41.
3. *Invasion from Mars*, Dell Publishing Co., New York, 1949. An anthology of 'interplanetary stories' selected and introduced by Welles. Also included is Howard Koch's radio script for *The War of the Worlds*.
4. *Une Grosse Légume*, Gallimard, Paris, 1953. A novel, translated by Maurice Bessy.
5. *Mr Arkadin*, Gallimard, Paris, 1954. A novel, first published in French and subsequently published in translation by W. H. Allen, London, 1956; Thomas Y. Crowell, New York, 1956; and Pyramid Books (paperback), New York, 1958. In a 1966 *Variety* interview, Welles stated that he had not done the translation, which is uncredited.
6. *This Is Orson Welles* by Peter Bogdanovich in collaboration with Orson Welles, Harper and Row, New York, 1972.

B. Plays by Welles

1. *Marching Song*, a five-act play on the life of John Brown by Welles and Roger Hill, *c.* 1933. Unpublished; existence unknown.
2. *Bright Lucifer*, two-act play, *c.* 1933, unpublished typescript with written corrections, in collection of the Wisconsin State Historical Society, Madison.
3. *His Honor the Mayor*, in *The Free Company Presents . . .*, Dodd & Mead, New York, 1941. A radio play first broadcast over CBS in 1941. Reprinted in *Playwrights Present Problems of Everyday Life*, edited by H. H. Giles and R. J. Carlson, 1942.

4. *Columbus Day*, radio play by Welles, R. Metzer, and Norris Houghton, in *Radio Drama in Action*, edited by Erik Barnouw, 1945.
5. *Fair Warning*, in *A Bon Entendeur*, Editions de la Table Ronde, Paris, 1953. A two-act play translated by Serge Greffet.
6. *Moby Dick – Rehearsed*, drama in blank verse and prose based on Herman Melville's novel, Samuel French, New York, 1965. Welles wrote the play in the early 1950s.

C.   Published scripts by Welles

1. *The Magnificent Ambersons*, in French, extracts printed in *La Revue du Cinéma*, 1946, and in *Premier Plan*, 1961.
2. *Citizen Kane*, in French, *L'Avant Scène du Cinéma*, 1962.
3. *Touch of Evil* and *The Trial*, in Spanish, *Temas de Cine*, 1962.
4. *The Trial*, in French, *L'Avant Scène du Cinéma*, 1963.
5. *Salomé*, in French, extract from an unproduced script printed in Maurice Bessy's *Orson Welles*, Paris, 1963.
6. *The Bible . . . in the Beginning*, Pocket Books, Inc., New York, 1966. Welles wrote the Abraham episode, which he had been planning to direct, but refused credit when the ending was changed in John Huston's film. Christopher Fry is the credited Author.
7. *The Trial*, dialogue transcription and description of action by Nicholas Fry, Simon and Schuster, New York, 1971.
8. *Citizen Kane*, edited and introduced by Pauline Kael in *The 'Citizen Kane' Book*, Little-Brown, Boston, 1971. Introduction reprinted from *The New Yorker*.

D.   Articles by Welles

1. 'Experiment', *The American Magazine*, November 1938.
2. 'To Architects', *Theatre Arts*, January 1939; reply to a questionnaire.
3. 'On Staging Shakespeare and on Shakespeare's Stage', introduction to *The Mercury Shakespeare*, Harper and Bros., London and New York, 1939.
4. '*Citizen Kane* is not About Louella Parsons' Boss', *Friday*, 14 February 1941. Also printed in the issue are a letter from Welles to Dan Gillmor of *Friday* and captions by Welles for stills from *Kane*. Article reprinted in *Film Focus on 'Citizen Kane'*, 1971.
5. 'Biography of William Shakespeare (No. 1,000,999)', with Roger Hill, *Scholastic*, 14 April 1941. A reprint of the preface to *Everybody's Shakespeare* and *The Mercury Shakespeare*.
6. Series of articles in *The New York Post* and *The Farmer's Almanac*, 1942–5.
7. Series of articles in *Free World*, New York: 'Moral Indebtedness', October 1943; 'Unknown Soldier', December 1943; 'Good Neighbor Policy Reconsidered', March 1944; 'Habits of Disunity', May 1944; 'Race Hate Must

be Outlawed', July 1944; 'War Correspondents', August 1944; 'American Leadership in '44', September 1944; 'Liberalism – Election's Victor', December 1944; 'G.I. Bill of Rights', January 1945; 'In Memoriam: Mankind Grieves for our late President', May 1945; 'Now or Never', September 1945.

8. Preface to *He That Plays the King*, by Kenneth Tynan, London, 1950.
9. 'Thoughts on Germany', *The Fortnightly*, London, March 1951.
10. Preface to *Les Truquages au Cinéma*, by Maurice Bessy, Paris, 1951.
11. Preface to *Précis de Prestidigitation*, by Bruce Elliott, Editions Payot, Paris, 1952.
12. Series of reflections in *La Démocratie Combattante*, Paris, April–May 1952.
13. Preface to *Put Money in Thy Purse*, by Micheál MacLiammóir, London, 1952.
14. 'The Third Audience', *Sight and Sound*, London, January–March 1954, reprinted in Peter Cowie's *The Cinema of Orson Welles*.
15. 'Je combats comme un géant dans un monde de nains pour le cinéma universel', *Arts*, Paris, 25 August 1954. Reprinted in translation as 'For a Universal Cinema', *Film Culture*, New York, Vol. 1, No. 1, January 1955.
16. 'Tackling *King Lear*', The New York *Times*, 8 January 1956.
17. Letter to Herman G. Weinberg, printed in *Film Culture*, Vol. 2, No. 4 (10), 1956, concerning *Mr Arkadin*.
18. 'The Scenario Crisis', *International Film Annual*, No. 1, London, 1957.
19. Letter to *The New Statesman*, London, 24 May 1958, concerning *Touch of Evil*.
20. 'Un ruban de rêves', *L'Express*, Paris, 5 June 1958, reprinted in translation as 'Ribbon of Dreams', *International Film Annual*, No. 2, London, 1958.
21. 'The Artist and the Critic', *The Observer*, London, 12 July 1958. Reprinted in *Notes and Counter Notes*, Writings on the Theatre by Eugène Ionesco, Gallimard, Paris, 1962, and Grove Press, Inc., New York, 1964.
22. '*The War of the Worlds*', *Action!*, Hollywood, May–June 1969. Transcript of Welles's remarks on Dean Martin's television show.
23. 'But Where Are We Going?', *Look*, New York, 3 November 1970.
24. Letter to *The Times*, London, 17 November 1971, concerning the script of *Citizen Kane*.

Recordings

The Mercury Shakespeare. Various editions of radio plays. CBS Records.
The War of the Worlds. The Mercury radio programme. Audio Rarities, LPA 2355; two-record set, Evolution Records, 4001.
Song of Myself. The Whitman poem, read on BBC radio. Westminster Recording Co., WBBC-8004.
No Man Is an Island. Readings from Pericles, Donne, Paine, Patrick Henry, Carnot, Daniel Webster, John Brown, Lincoln, and Zola. Decca Records, DL 9060.

The Finest Hours and *A Man for All Seasons*. Film soundtrack recordings.
The Begatting of the President. Reading of a satire by Myron Roberts, Lincoln Haynes, and Sasha Gilien. Mediarts Records, 41–2.

Unrealized film projects

The history of Welles's career is riddled with unmade films, some of them possibly only pipe-dreams (as John Houseman has remarked, 'Orson has established proprietary rights on film versions of most of the world's classics'), and some, like *Catch-22*, which pained him terribly not to direct. Before making *Citizen Kane*, he prepared *Heart of Darkness* and Nicholas Blake's *The Smiler With the Knife* for RKO. After *Kane*, he wanted to make *The Pickwick Papers*. During World War II, Alexander Korda announced that he would have Welles direct *War and Peace* when the war ended. In 1944 Welles proposed that Charlie Chaplin play Landru in a film he would direct; when Chaplin decided he wanted to direct the film himself, Welles protested, and Chaplin wound up giving him several thousand dollars and screen credit for the idea of *Monsieur Verdoux*. Other failed projects include: *Around the World in Eighty Days*, which he adapted for the stage but lost to Mike Todd on the screen; *Moby Dick*, which he had to abandon when John Huston made the film with Welles as Father Mapple; *The Odyssey*, which Ernest Borneman spent several months scripting for him; *Julius Caesar*, which he has announced for filming several times, shelving the project when John Houseman began his 1953 production and reviving the idea again in 1967, when it was announced that he would film it in modern dress; an original comedy, *Operation Cinderella*, about the postwar 'occupation' of an Italian town by a Hollywood movie company; three Bible stories – *Salomé* (for Korda), with himself as Herod; *Two by Two*, the story of Noah; and the Abraham episode of *The Bible*, which he wrote but refused to direct when the producers insisted that he not have Isaac resist the knife; and *Catch-22*, which he tried for years to buy before Mike Nichols made the film and cast him as General Dreedle. Projects still pending include *Midnight Plus One*, an adaptation of Gavin Lyall's novel which Welles will direct for BBS Productions, and *King Lear*. When an interviewer asked him in 1965 what films he really wanted to do, Welles replied, 'Mine. I have drawers full of scenarios written by me . . . I do not work enough. I am frustrated, do you understand?'

Acknowledgements

My debts are many, and without the encouragement of several people I would never have finished this book. Orson Welles gave generously of his time and attention to meet with me. Peter Bogdanovich, his collaborator on the book *This Is Orson Welles*, graciously compared notes. I would also like to thank William Donnelly and Michael Wilmington for their discussions of Welles and of everything else in general; Andrew Sarris and Robin Wood, two exceptional critics, for teaching me the trade; Jon Zwickey for his unique perception of Welles and his other insights; Andrew Holmes, Wayne Merry, Thomas Flinn, John Davis, Mark Bergman, and Gene Walsh, for helping me screen movies; Herman G. Weinberg, for his kindness; Edward F. Jost and Gerald Peary, for inviting me to speak about Welles; Marie Garness, devotee of Welles, for her enthusiasm; Wayne Campbell, for a pleasant afternoon of research; Penelope Houston, Tony Macklin, and Ernest Callenbach, for their editorial guidance; Tom Book, Candy Cashman, Ellen Whitman, Mark Goldblatt, Richard Thompson, Dave Shephard, Milton Luboviski, Jane Mankiewicz, Russell Merritt, and Larry Cohen, for their advice and interest; Steven Wonn, for his hell-raising; my parents and parents-in-law, for keeping the faith; and the members of the Wisconsin Film Society, for watching all those movies.

Stills by courtesy of RKO, Columbia, Hunter Films, Planet, 20th Century-Fox, United Artists, Universal, Warner Bros., Museum of Modern Art, State Historical Society of Wisconsin, Larry Edmunds Cinema Bookshop, Felipe Herba, and the Stills Library of the National Film Archive.

Sections of this book have appeared previously, some in slightly different forms, in *Film Quarterly*, *Film Heritage* and *Sight and Sound*, and the editors' permission to reprint is gratefully acknowledged. Parts of Chapters 4, 5 and 12 appeared in *Persistence of Vision*, edited by Joseph McBride, Wisconsin Film Society Press, Madison, 1968.

This book is for my wife, Linda, and our daughter, Jessica.

J.M.